GUITAR CHORDS: FOR BEGINNERS

2 Manuscripts in 1 Book, Including: How to Play Chords and How to Play Guitar

Preston Hoffman

Table of Contents

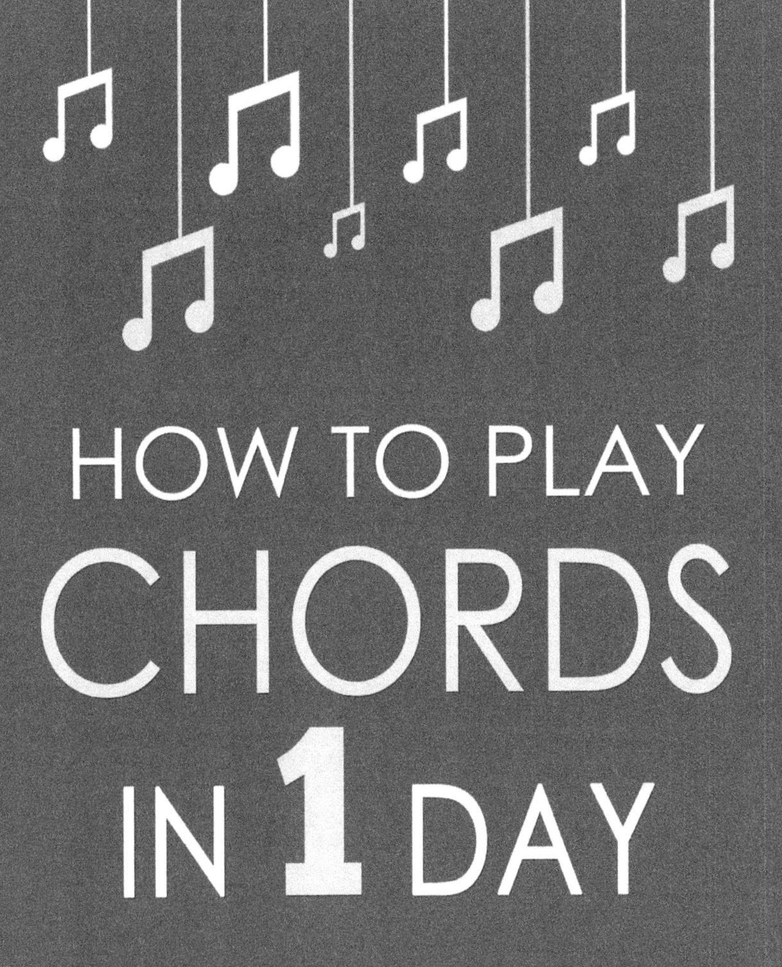

HOW TO PLAY
CHORDS
IN 1 DAY
The Only 7 Exercises You
Need to Learn Guitar Chords, Piano
Chords and Ukulele Chords Today
PRESTON HOFFMAN

BOOK 1

HOW TO PLAY CHORDS: IN 1 DAY

The Only 7 Exercises You Need to Learn Guitar Chords, Piano Chords and Ukulele Chords Today

Preston Hoffman

Table of Contents

Chapter One: Know Your Instruments

Welcome to your handy-dandy guide to learning how to play chords on the guitar, ukulele, and piano! It may come as a surprise—or it may not—to learn that all three of these instruments are quite easy to learn and you can quickly play thousands of songs on them just by following a few simple exercises and learning about the basic chords. But first, we need to break down the differences between these three instruments, since playing them will be slightly different for the chords and for your hands.

The Guitar

The guitar is the world's most popular instrument, and for good reason. It's versatile, easily portable, works well with other instruments, and is easy to learn—as you're about to find out. It has a wide range and is great for people who also enjoy singing, since you can easily play the guitar while you sing and it accompanies voices well.

There are many different types of guitars, the two main categories being acoustic and electric. It's recommended that you start with an acoustic guitar.

This here is an acoustic guitar:

And this is an electric guitar:

But there are variations within that, as well, like nylon versus steel strings, for example. Nylon strings are more mellow and easier on your fingers, while steel strings produce a bright tone and are louder. They're also harder on your fingers.

These here are nylon strings:

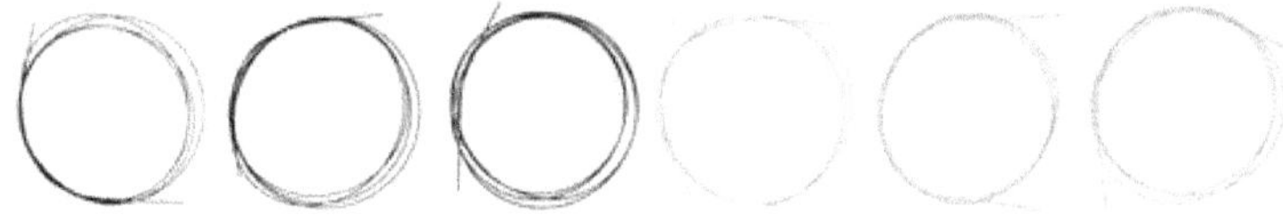

And these here are steel strings:

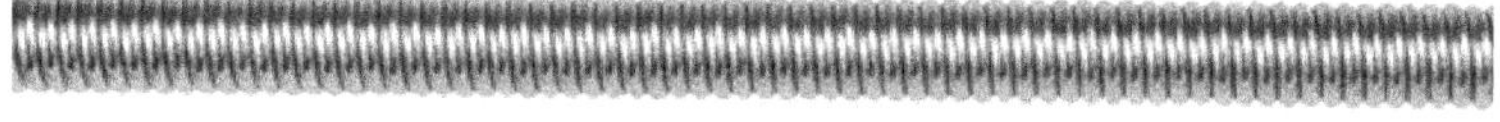

If those two images don't look too different to you, it's because the nylon is wrapped in either bronze-plated copper or in silver wire. If you're just looking at strings on a guitar, you might not be able to tell the difference at first. But you'll feel the difference in your fingers when you play them.

The best type of guitar for a beginner is a steel-strung guitar with round holes in the sideboards. They're the best for playing most of the songs you'll come across, including all of the songs in this book, and they create a good sound for accompanying singers and other instruments.

Another type of guitar is the Jumbo Guitar. It has an extra-large body, which means that it produces a better bass sound. If you're a bass player in a band, this might be the type of guitar you'd go for. This is a great guitar but with twelve strings and a larger body, it's not good for beginners:

It can be hard to see in this image, but where on a regular acoustic guitar like the one above each of the notches only has one string, these have two. Definitely not easy on your hands and the added musical value won't be of use to you until much later when you're further down the line in your understanding of music and can start to play around with the melodies of your songs instead of just focusing on the chords, which is what we're doing in this book.

Flamenco and Classical Guitars are strung with nylon and are used specifically for flamenco and classical music, respectively. They're good guitars and easy to learn on as a beginner but since they're for specialized music, you won't want to use them unless you're planning on playing mainly classical music.

There might not seem to be much of a difference in these guitars when you look at them, but it's all in the tuning. Flamenco guitars are designed to have a higher note register and the strings are therefore slightly different to accommodate this. Regular acoustic guitars have a lower register.

A classical guitar, on the other hand, will have a wider fret board, which can make it difficult for newer players to reach all of the strings, and they don't always have fret markers to help you out. Classical guitars just aren't designed for modern-day pop songs. Trying to play a Beatles song, for example, or that guitar classic "Wonderwall" on a classic guitar would just make it sound weird. So for our purposes, unless you want to play more classical music or more folk-sounding music, stick to regular acoustic.

Note: "Wonderwall" is considered one of the most overplayed songs on guitar, so it's best to avoid playing it.

Finally, electric guitars are the kind of guitars that can only be played when you plug them into an amplifier. You can attach pedals and other instruments to help play around with the sound of them. They're great for jazz and rock, but they might not be a good bet for a beginner. If you know your way around a guitar and want to start picking up some fancy tricks, new ways to play with sound, or you're joining a band and want to be able to be heard, then you can get an electric guitar.

Be sure to take good care of your guitar! Buy a sturdy case for it and store it in there. Hang onto the receipt after you buy it in case you're traveling with it and need to show the receipt to customs. Never let your guitar lie in the grass or dirt and be careful with it around moisture.

The Ukulele

There are, as you can tell just by looking at them, a lot of similarities between a ukulele and a guitar. However, there are also some differences to keep in mind.

First, there are the four types of ukulele: soprano, alto, tenor, and baritone—yes, just like singing voices. The soprano is the smallest, and the easiest to start out with as a beginner, since it has only four strings. The baritone is the largest and most expensive, and personally, if you're looking at a baritone then at that point you might just want to get a guitar instead.

Here is a soprano ukulele:

Here is an alto ukulele:

This is a tenor ukulele:

And finally, a baritone ukulele:

The ukulele will always sound a bit higher than the guitar, so it's natural when you're learning a song on the ukulele versus guitar for it to sound a bit higher—but the notes should still sound *right*. You'll find that it's easy for your ear to pick up the difference between notes played correctly at a higher pitch and notes that are played incorrectly. Fortunately, it's actually simpler to play chords on a ukulele than a guitar, so now that we've got you on the guitar, you'll find the transition to ukulele is pretty easy.

The most notable difference in a ukulele versus a guitar will be the strings. The tuning for a ukulele is usually GCEA:

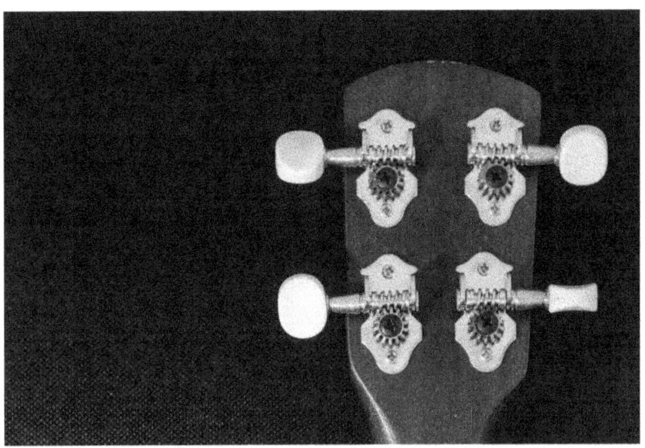

To compare this to a guitar, put a capo on the 5th fret of a guitar. A "capo" is a bar that you can buy that will hold down all of the strings on a particular fret for you. This will come in handy when you've progressed further and are performing songs where you're doing chords but can't have a finger free to hold down all the strings. With the capo on the 5th fret, play the four highest strings on your guitar. That's what it's like to play a ukulele, except that the G string on the ukulele is an octave higher even than that.

Baritone ukuleles, however, are exactly the same as the four highest strings on the guitar, no capo needed. This is why it's probably best not to buy a baritone ukulele—any song that you'd play on there you can just play on the guitar by ignoring the two lowest strings.

The Piano

The piano is probably the best known, and most beloved, of all musical instruments. Many composers started composing their pieces on piano to start with, before adding in the other instruments, and it's a versatile instrument that can handle pretty much any song that you throw at it.

A piano is, technically, a string instrument. When you press down on a key, you're actually starting up a mechanism that causes the string or strings to be plucked, causing the sound. It's also one of the most complicated instruments in the world, with 2,500 parts, and it's easily broken. The many parts of a piano include the soundboard, ribs, bridges, keys, pedals, hammers, the strings, and the cast iron plate.

Yes, a cast iron plate. It's put in over the soundboard of the piano and anchors the strings and keeps them tense so that they will vibrate properly when plucked by the hammer, which is caused by pressing on a key. The largest kind of piano is the grand piano:

These are also known as winged pianos and are the largest in size. You would need a rather large home to fit one of these. The next smallest is the baby grand piano, structured in every way like a grand piano, only with smaller dimensions:

The other kind of piano, and the one that most people can afford both economically and size-wise, is an upright piano:

And finally, we have the electric keyboard, the least expensive and most convenient for when you're living in a small house:

Unless you're living in an area where you have access to a grand or a baby grand, you don't need to worry about practicing on one. Practicing on a keyboard or upright piano will give you the same kind of understanding and practice, and if you're looking to perform, those are the two kinds of pianos that you'll most likely be performing on when the time comes.

Now that you understand your instruments, it's time to learn how to play them!

Chapter Two: What are Chords?

Chords are the basis for an entire song or piece of music. Without chords, you don't have a song, which is why if you know the chords of a song, you can play those same four or so notes over and over again in the rhythm of the song without learning the rest, and the audience will still recognize said song. By learning the chords through the exercises this book will teach, you'll be able to play thousands of songs. But what exactly are chords and how do they work?

What Is a Chord?

A chord is a combination of three or more notes. They're built off of a single note, known as the 'root note.' The root note will always be the first note in the chord sequence. So if you see the chord sequence C-E-G, that's a C chord. Those three notes together create a harmonious, blended sound, called the chord. When you're playing chords, whether it's guitar or piano or ukulele, you create the song by keeping your fingers in the same position, just moving them slightly up or down—so you're always playing the same notes, just as a higher or lower pitch.

How to Read Guitar and Ukulele Chords

Reading guitar and ukulele music is a bit different than reading piano music. Piano tends to use sheet music—which is important to know as a guitarist, because you'll have to read sheet music a lot of the time. Sheet music is the foundation on which all music is written, even if that music is later translated into another form, like guitar tabs.

Guitar tabs function for guitar and ukulele the way sheet music does for a piano. In fact, you can read the tabs without actually having to learn sheet music. This is part of why it's so easy to learn guitar and ukulele (and you can transfer this knowledge to the piano, as we'll discuss shortly).

Tabs are, essentially, a visual representation of where the notes are on the guitar or ukulele that you should be playing:

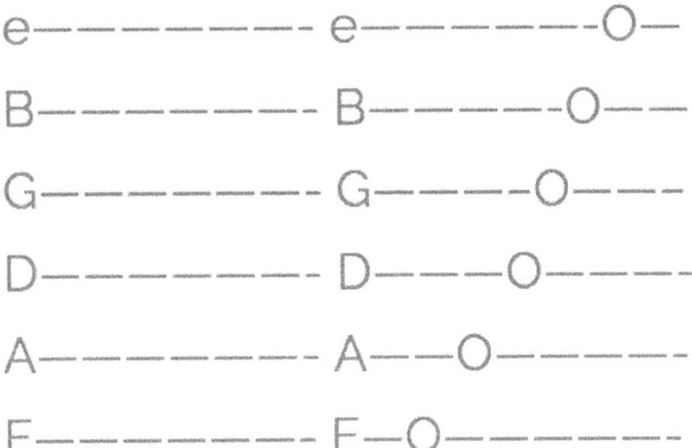

The strings on the guitar (if this was a ukulele, there would only be four strings) have the thickest, the E string, at the bottom, and the thinnest, the e string, at the top. If there is a number next to the letter, say, a 5 next to the D, that means you're placing your finger on the 5th fret of the D string. If there's a zero, that means the string is being played 'open' with no frets pressed down.

Look at that graphic again. A helpful way to remember the notes is to make an acronym for them. The one I learned was Every August Dogs Go Biting Elvis. E-A-D-G-B-E.

This is another diagram of how guitar chords might be written. The three black dots on the diagram show you which strings to press down—in this case, strings D, G, and B—and you will press down on them on the second fret. The E and A strings we're going to play open, without any frets pressed down, and the High E, or e, we're not going to play at all.

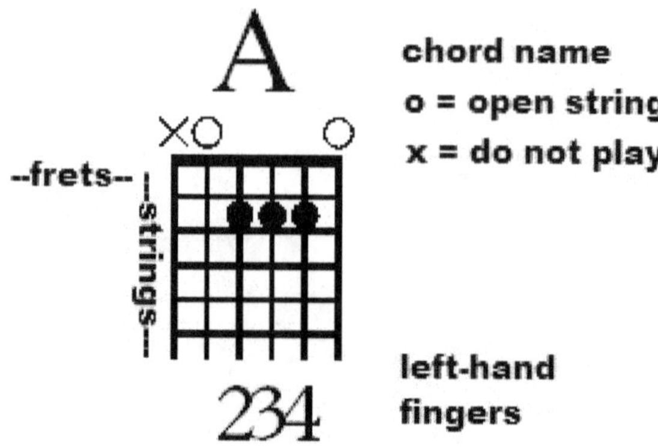

The numbers at the bottom of this chart are telling you which fingers to use to hold down the strings. Your index finger is number one, and your pinkie is number four. So for this, you'll use your middle, ring, and pinkie finger, and leave your index finger free. Keep in mind that your thumb doesn't come into play with the guitar. You use your thumb to brace against the back of the guitar so that it holds still while you move your other fingers. Here's an example of proper finger positioning:

Notice how the thumb is out of sight, bracing on the back of the guitar. The wrist is pushed forward which makes for an angle that will take some getting used to. The fingers, as you can see, are in position, so your index finger (number one) is stretching up to hit the top string.

Let's go back to that chart. So you'd put your middle finger, the 2 finger, on the D string, your ring finger, or 3 finger, on the G string, and your pinkie or 4 finger on the B string, all on the second fret. Use the tips of your fingers only! Otherwise you'll press down on other strings and the sound will come out muffled. Then strum with your other hand. Ta-da! You're now able to read a ukulele or guitar chart and figure out what to play.

The only difference in reading between a ukulele and a guitar is that there are only four strings on a ukulele, so there's just two fewer strings to worry about. But the finger positioning and how you read the chart is all the same.

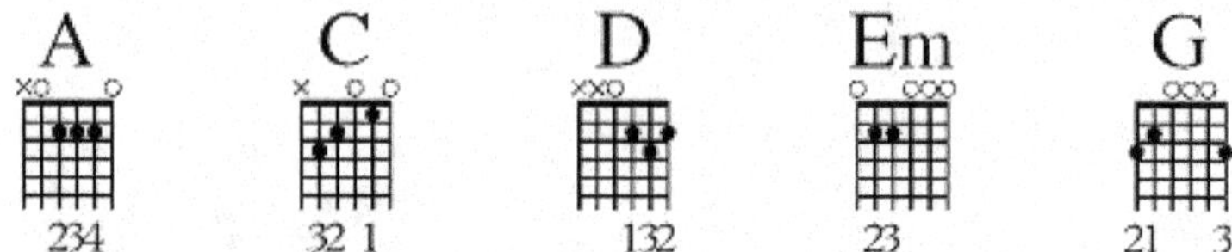

Take a look at these. We have the first one, the A chord, and now the C, D, Em, and G chords. Take a moment and figure out where your fingers go to practice reading it.

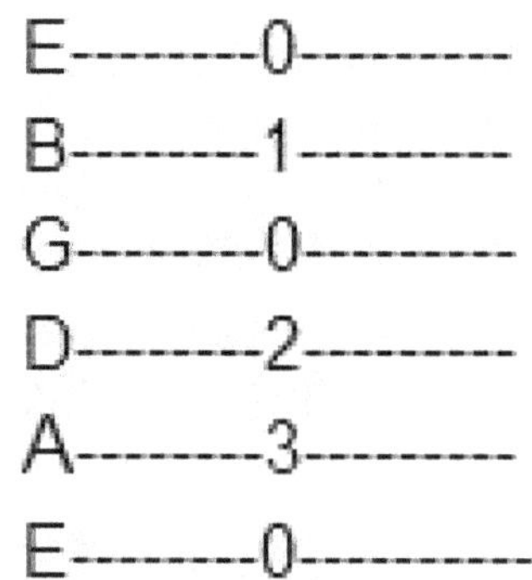

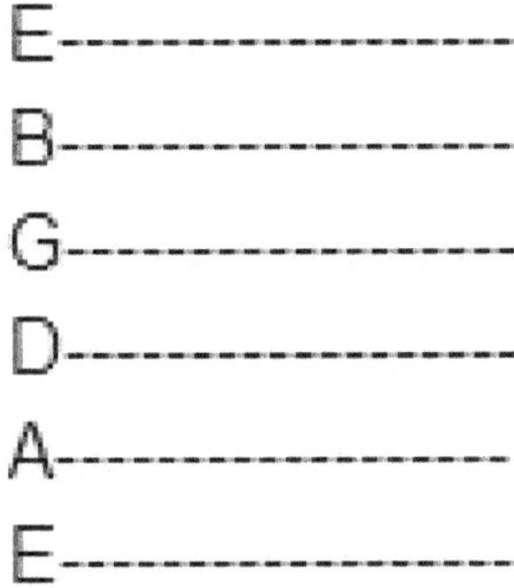

Now, look at the tabs again. The one on the right has no numbering. The one on the left has the numbering showing the fret you want to put your finger on. Unlike the previous chart, it doesn't tell you which finger—so we go with the basic principle of highest string goes to the index finger, second highest to the middle finger, and so on. For this one, you'd have your middle finger on the first fret of the B string, your ring finger on the second fret of the D string, and your pinkie on the third fret of the A string.

It's important to know these tabs because they'll help you for reading sheet music, and moving your chord exercises from guitar to the piano.

Piano Versus Guitar Chords

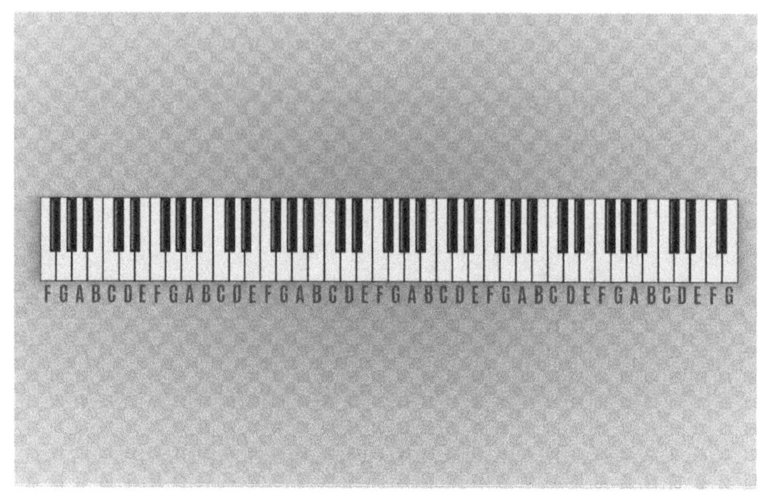

Ah, pianos. You've got a lot more room to work with than guitars, which is both a blessing and a curse when you're a beginner. Take a look at the image up above. Right away you'll notice that it has all of the notes laid out for you. Unlike a guitar, where you create the higher and lower notes by pressing down on the frets, the piano does that for you already. This means that you can play more complicated songs on the piano but it also means your fingers are going to be exhausted.

The key with playing the piano is to stretch your fingers and to keep your wrist light. This is very different from a guitar. In a guitar, if I were to grab your wrist and tug, your wrist shouldn't move. It should be firm to support the guitar neck and your fingers. A piano is the opposite—your wrist should be completely loose and relaxed to allow your fingers the most freedom of movement. If I were to press down on your wrist while you were playing piano, it should collapse.

Keep in mind as well that with both guitar and piano, each finger must move simultaneously. You will be fighting against instinct here. We have trained ourselves to treat our fingers as one unit, to pick things up, to throw things, and so on. Typing is arguably the only thing where our fingers move independently of one another. But look at this picture below:

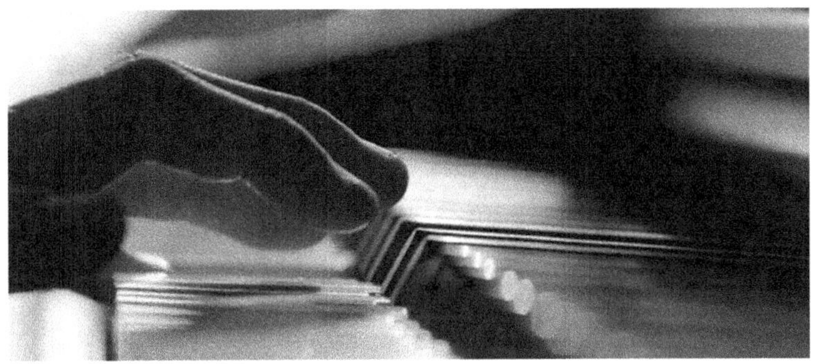

Note how the thumb is down on the keyboard but the other fingers are not. The thumb is moving independently of the others. If you move one finger on a piano or guitar, the other fingers shouldn't move at all.

Take a look at this picture:

Notice how the hands seem to dip down a little from the wrist, and the fingers are slightly curled. Like with guitar, you want your fingertips to be the ones making the notes, not your whole hand. See how relaxed the wrist is to allow the hand to droop like that? With the guitar, it's all about wrist strength. With piano, it's about wrist relaxation. But with both, remember, you need fingertips and finger flexibility.

Now, like guitar, a piano chord is any set of three or more notes played simultaneously. Note the image below:

The person's fingers are pressing down on keys while there is are white keys in between them. The thumb, middle finger, and pinkie of the person's right hand are pressing down on the white keys. This creates a chord the same way you do on a guitar. Most piano chords, and certainly these basic ones, will be made with your thumb, middle finger, and pinkie.

The person's left hand is doing the same thing—here is where you can get in some variation. In a guitar, for example, when you're playing the four or five notes with just your one hand, using all of your fingers. As you can see from the image above, those same four or five notes are played with both of your hands. Pressing down on the notes with both hands will create the chord for a piano, while strumming with one hand while the other holds down the strings creates the chord for a guitar or ukulele.

Now, fingers are numbered when you play piano, just like with the guitar. The only difference is that the thumb is included with piano, so instead of the index finger being number one, the thumb is number one, and you go on with the pinkie being number five. So most chords are 1-3-5 chords, using your thumb, middle finger, and pinkie, on three alternating notes.

Alternating is something you're going to come up against in both piano and guitar/ukulele. Now, there are half-steps and full-steps in notes. In a piano, a half-step is when you go from a white key to a black key, or vice versa. You're going from one note to the one directly above or below it. So if you're on the white key C, then go up to the nearest black key, C#, that's a half step. A full-step is where you go up two notes, or one 'full note.' You're not going up from a C to a C sharp or down to a C flat. It's just a full note, so from C to D—which is the next white key.

The only exception? When you're going from white key E. The F key is the same thing as an E#.

All you need to worry about, though, is that when making your chords go from guitar to piano, you put your thumb, or 1 finger, on the root note. Let's say it's C. You would then count up two full-steps. So you'd count up: C#, then D, then D#, then E. So you put your middle finger on E. Then count up two more full-steps: E, F/E#, then F#, to put your pinkie on G.

Now you have the C chord, C-E-G. This is called a major chord, by the way. A minor chord is the opposite. You would put your thumb on C, then go up only one full-step and one half-step, so you wouldn't go all the way up to E—you'd stop at D#. Then you'd put your pinkie on the same place, G. An easy way to remember this? Just put your fingers in position for the chord, then move your middle finger up one half-step.

This is an easy way to have fun with songs, by the way. Play any chord song, but move your middle finger up so that it's now in minor key. It'll sound cool and unusual and completely change how the song sounds.

Another way to help with figuring out the differences in your hands on the piano versus your one hand on the guitar is to imagine the three lowest guitar strings as what you play with your left hand on the piano, and the three highest strings as what you play with your right hand. So let's say you've got your five fingers on five strings on the guitar. Your left hand would take some of those notes, while your right hand would take the others, on the piano. You're just dividing up the notes in a different way, but you still play them all at the same time. A good rule of thumb is that your left hand on the piano plays the root note (so C, for C-E-G), and your right hand plays the others.

But what about sheet music?

That right there probably looks very intimidating. Never fear, though, you won't be learning any of that here—in fact, you won't have to. If you want to play more complicated, classical pieces, then you can learn those once you've mastered these basics, but we're here to learn chords that will allow you to sit down and play the songs that come on the radio. This will, in turn, give you the basic understanding that you'll need if you want to play these more complicated pieces but in the meantime, you'll make a killing serving as the human jukebox for your friends. So, sheet music!

This is a piece of blank sheet music. The first thing you should notice should already be familiar to you—the lines are just like the guitar strings on the guitar tabs we just learned. These lines are called the staff or staves, by the way. This is where you'll see the notes, rather like where you'll see the notations on the tab for which fret to hold down. However, unlike the tabs, which just tell you which fret, notes will tell you how long to hold the note for, so you can look at the sheet music and learn the rhythm even if you don't previously know the song.

This symbol here on the left is called a clef. This indicates the pitch of the notes that you're playing. F, C, and G are the usual types of clef. This here is a G clef, the one you'll probably recognize the most easily.

This here is an F clef.

And this:

Is a C clef. The G clef is the one that you'll come across the most often. You probably haven't even seen a C clef before. As you noticed in the image of the blank sheet music, there's a G and an F clef. A G clef is also known as a treble clef, and indicates higher notes, which is why it's higher on the lines. The F clef is also known as a bass clef and means lower notes. You won't often have to deal with such lower notes on your chords, not unless you choose to make your song lower in pitch.

But what are those symbols next to that image of the G clef? Those are 'key signatures.' They indicate how many sharps and flats are in a piece. You won't often need these but they can be helpful when you're going to play a chord to remember this when you're trying to remember which note is which that you're playing.

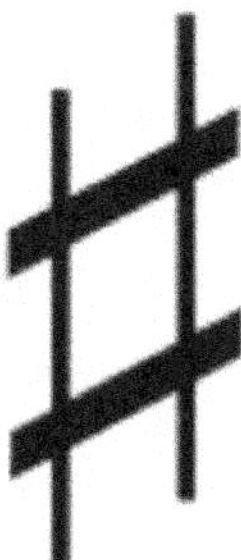

This symbol here is a sharp.

And this symbol is a flat.

Note that you'll run into sharps more than you'll run into flats. So if you're playing and you see a letter with one of these symbols after it, it will tell you to place your finger on the white key, and then either move it up a half-step to the nearest black key (a sharp) or down a half-step to the nearest black key (a flat).

The number of sharps and flats next to a clef will tell you what key the piece of music is in. The position of the flats and sharps tells you whether it's an F sharp or a G sharp or so on, and judging by how many there are and what position they're in you'll be able to know what key signature this is in.

This is helpful to keep in the back of your mind for playing classical pieces, but again, it's not necessary for knowing how to play the chords for songs.

Go back and look at the image of the blank sheet music again. You'll see that it ends at the edge of a page. This is called a bar. It will tell you that the measure, or period of time for this part of the music, is over. The number of beats per measure can vary, but there will be however many notes on the sheet music as there are beats, and then at the end there will be the bar. So if you're trying to figure out how many notes are in a measure, count the notations, and when you've reached the bar, you know how many there are—if you counted eight, then there are eight, and so on. The more notes, the faster the piece.

Unlike a guitar or ukulele, where you have to know the song to know how the rhythm goes, the piano music will tell you.

This is a whole note. You hold it four a count of four:

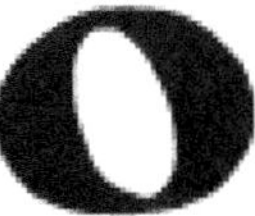

This is a half note. You hold it for a count of two:

This is an ordinary note. Technically it's a quarter note, but it's the most common note that you'll find. You hold it for a single beat:

Sometimes you'll run into these notes:

This dot serves as a half beat. Normally, you're multiplying and dividing by two—a quarter note is one beat, a half note is two beats, and a whole note is four beats. When you see a dot next to this, it means add half of the note's value. So this dot is next to a quarter note, meaning you add half a beat. If it were next to a half note, you'd add one beat, making the entire note three beats long.

This is an eighth note:

As you can imagine, eighth notes are very short, half a beat. They are always half a beat, unlike dots, which can change in value based on the note they're next to. A dot is half the value of the note it's next to, so the value of the dot changes depending on whether it's accompanying a quarter or whole or half note. An eighth note is always half a beat, no matter what other note it's with.

If you ever see a symbol like this:

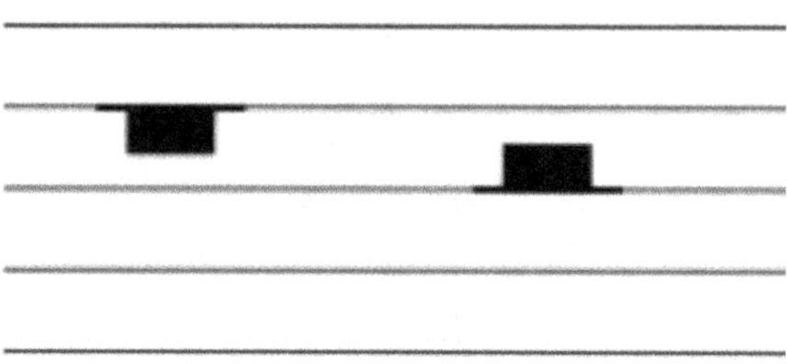

Whether it's facing up or down, that means it's a rest. Facing down, it's a whole rest, so four beats. Facing up, it's a half rest, or two beats.

These indicate shorter rests:

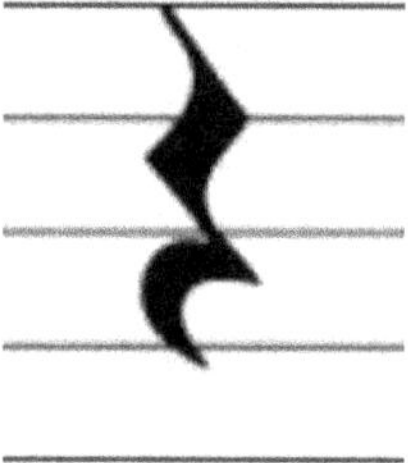

This is a quarter rest.

And this is an eighth rest. You count them just like you count the musical notes, but you don't play anything. These symbols stand for silence, and once again they indicate to you the rhythm of a piece.

Learning these basics of piano sheet music are helpful because while you can learn a song using guitar tabs for the guitar and ukulele, if you're ever unsure about the rhythm of a piece, you can look it up on sheet music and see how long each note is and figure out the rhthym.

Vocabulary

Here are some terms that you'll need to be familiar with, especially for piano, for when you pick up sheet music or if you are performing with others.

- Playing in Different Keys: This means that the position of your finger stays the same but the root note changes. For example, "I'm playing in F major instead of C major." Same chord position, but different notes, because you moved your fingers higher or lower on the guitar or piano.

- Arrangement: This is for if you're playing with a group. The arrangement decides who is playing what notes on the chord, which tempos, and when.
- Chord Extensions: This means adding alterations to a chord, which can make it sound completely different even if the basic notes are the same.
- Rhythm: This is how many pop songs can sound different even though they are all using the same chord. The rhythm is one of the first things that people notice when listening to a song, so changing it up can change the song almost completely.
- Melody: These are the varying notes that you play over the base chord—again, a way to take the same chord and make it sound different.
- Lyrics: You probably know this one already, but lyrics are the words that someone sings in time to the music.
- Adagio: This means to go slowly.
- Allegro: This means to play quickly.
- Beat: This is another word for rhythm.
- Leggiero: This is used mostly in piano, and means to play 'lightly' without putting too much force on the keys.
- Time Signature: How many beats are in each bar of music. So if there are eight beats, then the time signature is eight. The more beats, the faster you play.

- Bridge: A transitional passage. The repeated lyrics that a singer sings just before the chorus is the bridge—it literally 'bridges' the versus to the chorus.
- Chorus: The repeated phrase of the song, the heart of the song's meaning and music.
- Measure: One complete cycle of the time signature.
- Meter: This is the pattern of the rhythm. Think of it as the pauses in between the beats.
- Forte: To play strong and powerfully.
- Piano: This isn't the instrument—if someone says to play piano, it means to play it gently.
- Tempo: This is the overall speed of the piece. The meter and beat and rhythm make up the tempo.
- Rest Signs: This indicates when you stop playing your instrument and let it 'rest' for a period of time. This is usually done when you're playing with other instruments, so you all get your turn in the spotlight.
- Notes: The indication of what string or key you should be playing and for how long. Depending on the shape or shading of the note, it'll tell you how long to hold it for.

Chapter Three: The Seven Exercises

Now that you understand what your instruments are, how they work, how to read and understand music and bar chords, you're fully equipped to sally forth and play these instruments like a pro. Here are the seven basic exercises that will help you to play pretty much any song in the world.

Exercise One:

We're going to start with a C Major chord. This is the easiest chord to learn. Lots of songs, including "Are We Out of the Woods" by Taylor Swift and "Stay with Me" by Sam Smith use this key.

So, if you're on a guitar or ukulele, put your index finger on the first fret of the second string (B string). Then put your middle finger on the fourth string, on the second fret (this is the D string). Your ring finger goes on the third fret of the fifth string, or A string, and that's it! You don't play the sixth string, E, and the other two strings, e and G, are played open, so no fingers on those frets. Here's a picture of what that looks like on a guitar:

To play this on piano, you want to do these three keys that
are in red:

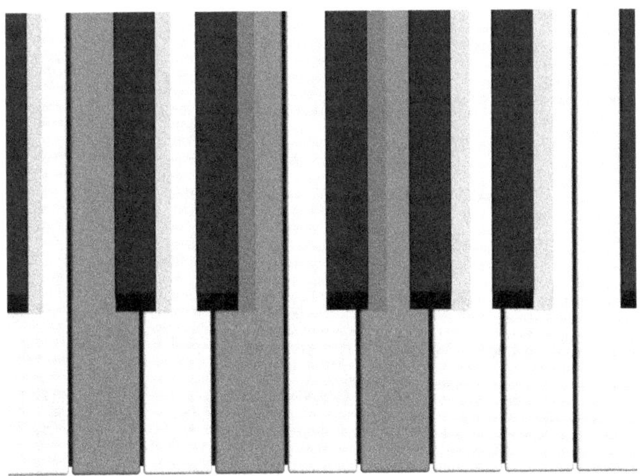

You can play them in any part of the piano, it's still the same chord. Practice doing it on the piano and on the guitar—remember to only strum five of the strings, not the E string—and on the ukulele, until you can do it in a steady rhythm of one, two, three, four.

To get an idea of how rhythm can completely change this song, do this chord while singing "Are We Out of the Woods" by Taylor Swift. You can play the song itself to accompany you if you feel more comfortable with that. Feel how fast that chord is. Then play "Stay with Me" by Sam Smith. This is very slow, with the chord playing, and then a long rest. That change in rhythm completely changes how the song feels.

Exercise Two:

Next exercise is the G major chord! "You Shook Me All Night Long" by AC/DC and "Heart of Gold" by Birdy are two G major chord songs, and again, very different in sound because of the rhythm.

Put your index finger on second fret of the fifth string, or A string. Then put your middle finger on the third fret of the bottom string, the E string. Your ring finger goes on the third fret of the e string, the first string, and your pinkie doesn't have to do anything. Keep in mind that your index and middle fingers have to be arched up so they don't accidentally brush other strings. This is where using your fingertips is important.

Here's an image of what your hand should look like:

Here is that same chord on the piano:

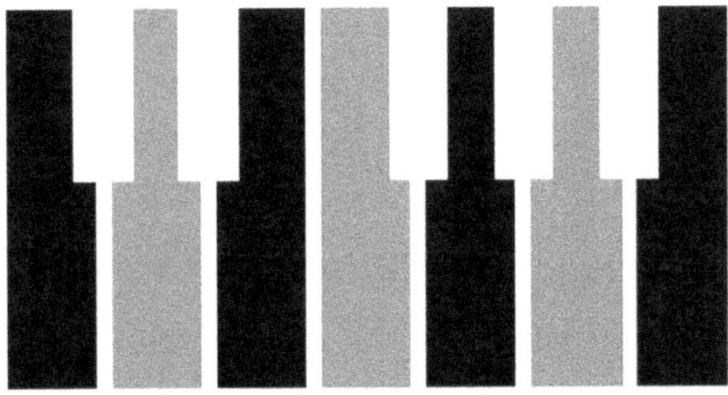

The red are the ones you want to be hitting. Use your
fingertips on your thumb, middle finger, and pinkie, so that you

don't hit any other keys while you're playing this. Again, practice just doing this on your guitar and piano and ukulele as just a one, two, three, four beat rhythm. Don't try to rush things. Try out the two songs, by Birdy and AC/DC, just to feel the difference the rhythm and the melody of the singer can do to change a song that has the same chords.

Exercise Three:

Next we're doing the D chord. This is an important chord on guitar for pop songs, so while you wouldn't normally learn it as quickly if you were studying piano for classical music, you're going to learn it here so that you can play all those songs on piano and guitar easily. Songs that use the D Major Chord include "Send My Love (to Your New Lover)" by Adele and "The Boys are Back in Town" by Thin Lizzy.

Put your index finger on the second fret of the fourth string, or G string. Then put your middle finger on the second fret of the sixth string, the e string, and then put your ring finger on the third fret of the fifth or B string.

If this chord seems a little more difficult for your fingers to handle on the guitar, that's how it should be. Some other very common chords that we're going to learn next are going to have four notes in them instead of just three, so this D major chord will help you, especially so that you can learn the F Major chord for the next exercise.

This is what this chord looks like on the guitar:

And this is what it looks like on piano:

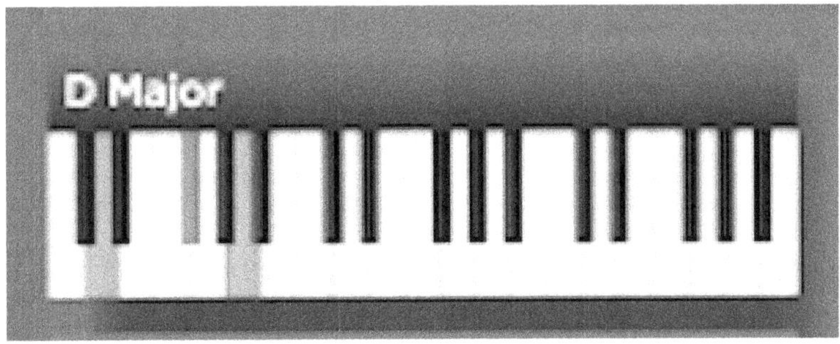

Notice that for this you're using one black key on the piano. Practice strumming on guitar or ukulele and getting the rhythm on the piano, using the two songs as accompaniment to help you if you feel you need it. Having a song in mind as your goal can be helpful as it helps you to integrate the idea of a rhythm into your playing.

Exercise Four:

Now we're getting into that F Major Chord that we mentioned. "Still Into You" by Paramore, "What's My Age Again?" by Blink-182, and "Ain't No Rest for the Wicked" by Cage the Elephant are all in this key. It's a popular one.

This is the first chord that uses four fingers on the guitar, and it's difficult because it's a bar chord. This means you have to take your index finger and put it down across the first fret on all of the strings. Yup, all of them. This will take some getting used to because your finger needs to build up the strength to hold all six strings (or four strings, for the ukulele) down at the same time.

Keep in mind that your finger shouldn't be directly on the fret. Rather, it should be directly behind the fret. So when you put your finger on, say, the second fret of the D string, your fingertip should actually be right before the line of the fret. This actually gives you less work to do as the fret can then do its job to hold the string in place and help it resonate. If you ever pluck a guitar string and it doesn't have a clear, resonating sound, it's probably because your finger is on the fret rather than behind it.

So, put your index finger across all the strings on the first fret. Then put your middle finger on the second fret of the third or G string, your ring finger on the third fret of the fifth or A string, and your pinkie on the third fret of the fourth or D string. This is how it should look on guitar:

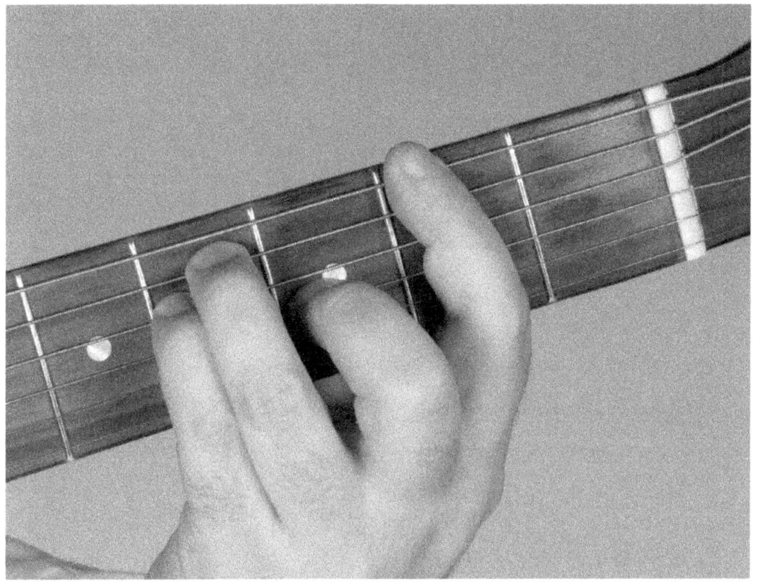

Notice how the index finger looks curved? You're going to have to do that in order to cover all of the frets while giving your other fingers the room to press on their strings.

On piano, however, this is one of the easiest chords. It looks like this:

You don't even have to stretch your fingers. Practice with this chord as well and get the feel for it.

Exercise Five:

We're going to get really fancy now. This exercise, you're going to practice doing a chord progression.

Songs progress from one chord to another, generally in four sets. So you'll have four sets of three or four notes that you repeat, over and over again. Take the F Major Chord that we just used. You won't keep your fingers on the same fret the entire song, but you will keep them in the same position. You just slide your hand up or down to hit different notes. Same with a piano. To play the full song, you keep your fingers in the same position and just move your and up or down the keyboard or neck of your guitar and ukulele.

For example, for "Ain't No Rest for the Wicked" by Cage the Elephant, you get your hands into the F major position. You start on the third fret. Then move your hand until the index finger is on the fifth fret. Now move it so your index finger is on the eighth fret. Now move your index finger to the first fret. Now back down to the third fret.

You've now just played the entirety of the song, all without moving your fingers, just sliding your hand up and down and strumming to the beat. Do that with all of the songs on guitar and piano and ukulele: find the notes on the sheet music and move your hands up and down until you've got it all down.

Exercise Six:

So, our next mission: practicing those chord progressions. Let's take a look at this handy dandy chart:

See how you can look at the notes both on piano sheet music, on the charts, and on guitar tabs? Chord progressions are often written in roman numerals. So G major is I, and C major is IV.

The list of progressions at the bottom is what you need to practice. You switch your fingers from chord to chord. Start just with the four that you know. The I-V-vi-IV chord progression, or G-D-em-C, is one of the most common in pop music. The only difference is the rhythm and which one of these four you start on, but it's the same order. So if you start on C, the next three notes are G, D, and em, then back to C again. If you start on D, then it's em, C, and then G before back to D. If you just practice going through these four, going slowly, then you can find you're playing pretty much every pop song that you know.

What's a metronome, you ask? This handy-dandy little thing:

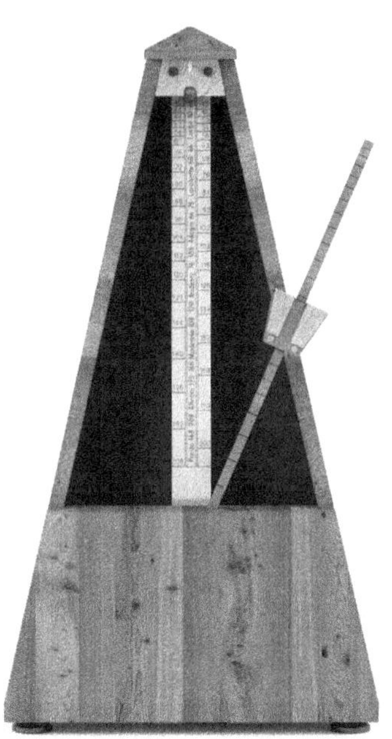

You can get a version on your phone or computer if you don't want to buy one. It keeps time for you. Put it on a slow setting and try to strum, or if you're on piano press down, in time with the metronome. This will help you improve your sense of rhythm while you do these chord progressions.

It's okay if you can't get all of these chord progressions right away. But by now your fingers will have gotten used to the positions on the piano and on the guitar, and you can always go back to the earlier exercises if you need. Just keep following these chord progressions until you're able to move back and forth smoothly between them.

Exercise Seven:

Here are some more chord progressions, this time in E major! What is E major for guitar and piano? It's a little more difficult, so here are some visuals:

You want your index finger on the fourth string on the first fret, your middle finger on the second string on the second fret, and your ring finger on the third string, also in the second fret—which is where it gets tricky, since you're having two fingers share that same space and need to press down on both strings in the same place. Your pinkie can stay out of the way. "Back in

Black" by AC/DC and "Pour Some Sugar on Me" by Def Leppard are two songs in the key of E Major.

Here's what it looks like on piano:

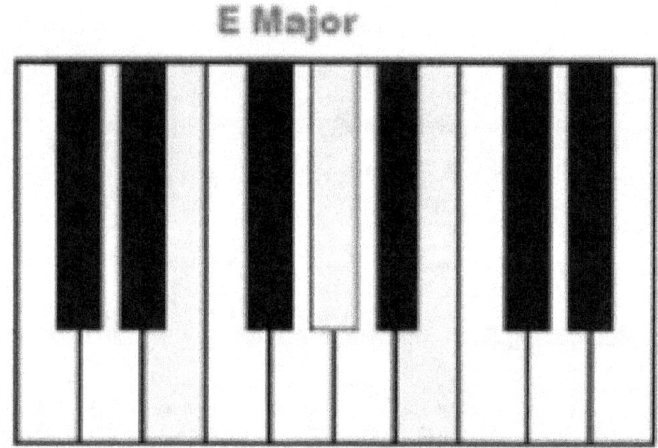

Again, much easier on piano than on guitar. You'll find that most of these chord progressions are easier to do on the piano rather than on guitar or ukulele, whereas reading sheet music for piano is harder than reading tabs and charts for guitar. It's a give and take, but both instruments are easily translatable into the other.

Here are the chord progressions for E Major:

Look at it as a chart, as a tab, as sheet music, and as roman numerals. The more you practice, the more you'll be able to just look at any one of these and understand. Go through the chord progressions on this sheet, and the previous one, and you'll know pretty much everything there is to know about playing basic songs by the time that you're through.

It's almost unbelievable how easy it is to pick all of this up—constant practice is the key, but with these fundamentals, you'll be wowing your friends and family in no time. In the next chapter, we'll explore some tips to keep in mind not just as you do these exercises but as you progress further.

Chapter Four: Tips for Practicing

So now we're going to go over some random tips that'll help you out as you're practicing. Keep in mind that everyone learns just a little bit differently, so what might work for one person won't work for you. But these are all things to keep in mind as you practice the seven exercises:

Tip #1:

Practice doing your chord shapes one finger at a time, if you're having trouble remember where to keep all of your fingers. Starting with just one finger at a time can help take the pressure off and keep you from getting confused. There's no harm in starting slow.

Tip #2:

Practice the chord shapes without strumming. Again, no harm in starting slow if that's what you need. The key here is to get those chords memorized so that you can play any song that you want, so don't rush forward if you don't have those.

Tip #3:

Pay attention to the chord changes. Transitions are the hardest thing to get down, so you'll want to practice those a lot. It'll seem hard at first, switching the positions of your fingers, more so on guitar than on piano since you're bending your wrist into an odd shape. With piano, the struggle will be teaching your fingers how to stretch out. But don't get discouraged! Practice transitions.

Tip #4:

Keep your metronome slow. I know, you want to go fast! And you'll be surprised by how fast even the slower songs feel once you start playing them. Getting these exercises down is what matters, not the speed.

Tip #5:

Make a practice plan and stick to it. This can go both ways—don't overbook yourself, but don't sell yourself short, either. Plan for a good amount of time that works easily with your schedule. Otherwise you'll find yourself making excuses. Say, for example, you've planned to practice for an hour every day. But when you get home from work, you find that the idea of practicing for a whole hour is just too draining. So you make excuses to not do it, thinking you'll make up the time later. Or, conversely, say you've promised yourself that you'll practice for ten minutes a day—and then get frustrated when you're not making a lot of progress. Find a time that isn't too ambitious but still gives you a good solid bit to practice your exercises.

Tip #6:

Find a chord dictionary so that when you've progressed beyond the more basic chords of these songs you can learn new ones and keep in practice. It's amazing the amount of chords and chord variations that are out there, and once you've mastered these, you can get really fancy and wow everyone. This is especially true of piano—once you've mastered these exercises and chords, go ahead and get a beginner's piano book with some classical pieces in it. You'll be surprised at how many you'll be able to play!

Tip #7:

It's important to keep your fingers and wrists healthy. Remember that with piano, your wrist is supposed to be completely relaxed, and your fingertips have to do a lot of stretching but remain light. With guitar and ukulele, your wrist has to be strong and in position, and your fingertips have to be strong to put the right amount of pressure on the strings. It can be easy for you to hurt your fingers and wrists over time if you don't do proper exercises. Take time to bend your wrists, rotate them, clench and unclench your fist (a small exercise ball is good for this) and practice lifting and extending your fingers and holding the position. It might seem silly, but doing these exercises before you play will help to prevent hand cramps and wrist pain later on. Below is an example of some wrist exercises that you can to do help keep your wrists flexible, strong, and healthy. A ten-minute warm up for your fingers and wrists might very well seem silly, but carpel tunnel syndrome and other health hazards have seriously affected the performance of guitarists and pianists for years, including famous ones. It's better to do some warming up than to spend months in pain and unable to practice.

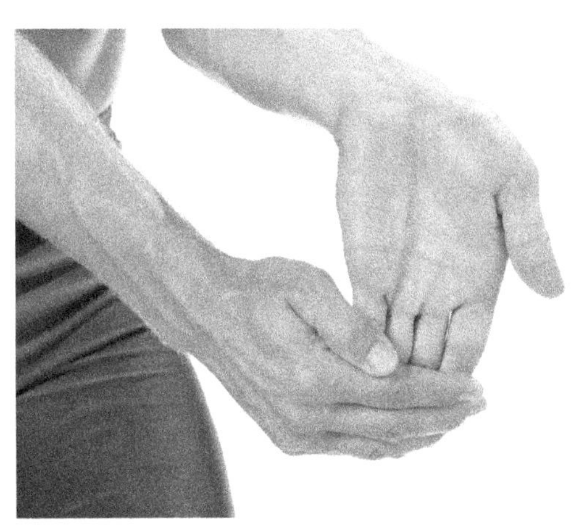

Tip #8:

If you find yourself getting frustrated or tired, or like you want to smash your piano to bits, then take a break. Walk away and get some fresh air. You won't learn if you find yourself hating practice, so go easy on yourself!

Tip #9:

Regular practice is better than how much you practice. Practicing for twenty minutes a day is better than practicing for two hours once a week. You want the repetition to get into your fingers.

Tip #10:

Count out loud as you practice your rhythms when you're doing these chords. It might sound silly, but it helps you to integrate the rhythm into your head. Some prefer, for example, to count using numbers. Others use phrases corresponding to the notes on the sheet music: "whole note hold it," for a whole note, or "quarter dot" for a quarter note with a dot on it. Whatever you use doesn't matter so long as you say it out loud to practice.

Tip #11:

Explore and have fun! Go onto the internet and find videos that show you how to play new songs. Go to a local jam session or open mike night at a café and perform for some people. Try writing your own songs or playing around with chord combinations. You learned these instruments because you wanted to, so don't lose sight of that. Do this for your own enjoyment.

Chapter Five: Moving Beyond the Basics

Ideas to keep in mind as you progress to more complicated chords, especially on the piano, and the idea of songwriting, and how these instruments can all play together at the same time.

Keep in mind chord changes and how they affect the song. You want your transitions to be smooth, for the sound to be clear and to resonate, and for you to get good at knowing where to place your fingers without having to pause and look.

Piano and guitar, and even ukulele, are great instruments for accompanying singers. You're going to get a lot of requests to accompany people when they want to sing a song, and you're probably going to want to sing a song yourself while providing your own accompaniment. As you gain confidence, you'll be tempted to really let your playing skills shine. Don't! The melody, and therefore the singer, is the star of the show. Practice playing at the right volume without too much energy so that you don't drown out the singer and steal the show, even if it's from yourself. After all, your chords are great but what if no one can hear what you're singing?

You're going to sometimes run into a problem where you have a piece on guitar tabs that you want to translate to piano sheet music, and vice versa. Doing this should wait until you've gotten comfortable with chord progressions and the exercises listed previously. You'll be able to figure out dozens of songs just by doing the chord progressions using different rhythms and accompanying a recording of a song (it can help to get an instrumental copy of said song, so the singer doesn't distract you with her melody). But when the time comes, here's a good example using the classic "Stairway to Heaven":

Tabs and sheet music are, fortunately, both on lines. So you would start by looking at what line the first note is on. It should say 7 and be on the third line from the bottom: the seventh fret of the D string. Now, you count backwards seven frets until you get to the open string—and count backwards on the piano at the same time. D, D#, E, F, F#, G, G#, and then ending on A. So the first note you'd play for this on the piano is A.

You just keep transcribing that way, counting backwards on the piano from how many frets there are on the guitar, to find each note. It's time consuming, but once you've moved past the beginning stages and want to learn more complicated songs like "Stairway to Heaven," you'll find yourself in this position a lot.

Piano can be especially difficult to learn as you progress further in your understanding of music. With the guitar, you'll want to start to simply incorporate the melody—this means plucking individual strings in between the strumming of the chords. But integrating the piano melody can take a lot of practice as you're moving both hands in different ways simultaneously. This is where fundamentals are important. Return to your chords when you feel frustrated and keep practicing those. Work on tapping each individual key out to improve your fingers' ability to move independently. And do the fundamentals like learn your scales. They're not necessary to learn for these chord songs, but if you want to move beyond that into more classical pieces, then you'll have to start learning them.

As you progress, you'll start to develop your own personal style. You might add a little flair to your version of "Don't Stop Believing" by Journey, or perhaps you moved your middle finger up to switch to a minor key for when you play "Hey, Jude" by the Beatles on the piano. That is totally right and natural to do. Embrace your personal style and as you grow in confidence, experiment. Experimenting on already-existing chords and chord songs is how new chord songs are made, so have at it.

If you want to start getting into songwriting, there are tons of ways that you can go about it. Tom Waits, a singer-songwriter, would play multiple radios at once to find where the songs overlapped in their chords. You might find that the chords of one song would match the riff of another, and combining them makes your own song.

Another way to do it is don't give yourself time to second-guess anything. Set a timer for fifteen minutes. You now have to get your song written in that time. Ready, set, go! This eliminates your ability to second-guess yourself and agonize over a particular chord. You never know what you'll find when you're racing against the clock.

And sometimes, just stop listening to music. Stare out the window for a while. Revel in the silence. Spend a day not talking, just listening to everything around you. Shutting off one of your sensory inputs or outputs, whether it's forcing yourself to just stare out of your skylight, promising yourself not to talk, or not listening to anything. Removing one sense can heighten the others and give your brain a chance to rest and see things in a new way that might give you the inspiration that you need.

If you've moved past the chord progressions and have learned the songs in this book and still want to go further, remember, you can always get yourself a teacher. Even if that 'teacher' is someone on the internet who posts videos about their work on ukulele or piano or whatnot, they can be a source of inspiration and added learning for you as you move farther along in your study of music. There's only so much that you can learn on your own without someone helping to walk you through the more complicated parts, so if you find yourself moving past the chord songs and want to challenge yourself, a teacher can be someone to help walk you through that.

Similarly to that, join in the conversation in the music world! Look up what musicians are saying about their work, listen to new songs, join a band, go listen to an open mike night. You can't operate in a vacuum and collaborating with others, even if that collaboration is just you sitting and listening, is an important part of the artistic process. Find a group of people that you can share ideas with and who you can learn from. You'd be surprised at how it helps improve not only your playing but your understanding of music in general.

Chapter Six: Chord Songs

Here is a list of different songs that you can play using the basic chords. Most of them use the most popular "pop music" chord that we previously discussed, but others use some of the six other chords. Now that you know the basic chords you can play any of these songs with ease—you just have to learn the tempo. One of my personal favorites, and the song that I started learning when I was a beginner, is "Ain't No Rest for the Wicked" by Cage the Elephant. If you're a little amazed by how many songs are on here, just think of how your friends will feel when you sit down at a piano or whip out your guitar or ukulele and find that you've turned into a musical genius. It's all in those basic chords.

Something to keep in mind is that the melody will vary from song to song. That's not actually what matters when playing the song, though. If you play the right chord, in the right rhythm, you'll actually be fine. In fact in a lot of bands, one guitar plays just the chords while the other plays the melody. If you have the chords down, the audience will know the song—especially if you're singing, because your voice then carries the melody so you don't have to worry about actually doing it with your guitar. Helpful, right?

I-V-vi-IV Songs:

The following songs are songs that are done using the most common chord, I-V-vi-IV. Many people have pointed out the use of this chord in pop songs, and while some would argue it's overused, this is good news for you because with this chord you can play hundreds of different songs using this one chord. Songs that use this chord include:

Don't Stop Believing by Journey

You're Beautiful by James Blunt

Forever Young by Alphaville

I'm Yours by Jason Mraz

Hey Soul Sister by Train

Wherever You Will Go by The Calling

Can You Feel the Love Tonight by Elton John (from The Lion King)

Take Me Home, Country Roads by John Denver

She Will Be Loved by Maroon Five

Let it Be by The Beatles

When I Come Around by Green Day

Save Tonight by Eagle Eye Cherry

Africa by Toto

Behind These Hazel Eyes by Kelly Clarkson

One of Us by Joan Osborne

Complicated by Avril Lavigne

Apologize by OneRepublic

Otherside by Red Hot Chili Peppers

Kids by MGMT

Superman by Five for Fighting

Going by Key:

Another way that you can look up songs is to look them up by the major chord. The following are songs divided by the chords that we learned in our exercises.

C Major Songs:

Happier by Ed Sheeran

Heaven by Bryan Adams

How Does it Feel by Avril Lavigne

Sweetest Devotion by Adele

When My Heart Beats Like a Hammer by B.B. King

Bang Bang by Ariana Grande

Stay with Me by Sam Smith

Are We Out of the Woods by Taylor Swift

Minority by Green Day

Stockholm Syndrome by Muse

Use Somebody by Kings of Leon

Wanted (Dead or Alive) by Bon Jovi

Stay by Rihanna featuring Mikky Echo

G Major Songs:

Under the Tide by Chvrches

Make You Feel Better by Red Hot Chili Peppers

Wake by Linkin Park

You Shook Me All Night Long by AC/DC

How Do We (Party) by Rita Ora

Shake it Off by Taylor Swift

Welcome to New York by Taylor Swift

Heart of Gold by Birdy

Been a Son by Nirvana

Whiskey in the Jar by Thin Lizzy

She's a Rebel by Green Day

Here I Go Again by White Snake

Little Wing by Jimi Hendrix

Sweet Home Alabama by Lynyrd Skynyrd

Wonderful Tonight by Eric Clapton

Call Me Maybe by Carly Rae Jepsen

I Gotta Feeling by The Black-Eyed Peas

Swing Swing by All-American Rejects

Good Riddance (Time of Your Life) by Green Day

Wake Me Up When September Ends by Green Day

D Major Songs:

Send My Love (To Your New Lover) by Adele

We Sink by Chvrches

Castle on the Hill by Ed Sheeran

Align by Nina Nesbitt

All is Now Harmed by Ben Howard

Lithium by Nirvana

Settle Down by The 1975

Home by Gabrielle Aplin

Grow Up by Paramore

Wake Up by Rage Against the Machine

Hysteria by Muse

Under the Bridge by Red Hot Chili Peppers

Times Like These by The Foo Fighters

Only Girl (In the World) by Rihanna

Love Story by Taylor Swift

Summer of '69 by Bryan Adams

Hey There Delilah by The Plain White Ts

E Major Songs:

Break My Heart by Hey Violet

Don't Tell Me by Avril Lavigne

All I Ask by Adele

Piano by Ariana Grande

Ain't it Fun by Paramore

Basket Case by Green Day

Buck Rogers by Feeder

Back in Black by AC/DC

Sex on Fire by Kings of Leon

Pour Some Sugar on Me by Def Leppard

Midnight Memories by One Direction

Fat Lip by Sum 41

I Believe in a Thing Called Love by The Darkness

F Major Songs:

Ain't No Rest for the Wicked by Cage the Elephant

I'm Not the Only One by Sam Smith

Blank Space by Taylor Swift

What's My Age Again by Blink-182

Party in the U.S.A. by Miley Cyrus

Still into You by Paramore

The Wind Cries Mary by Jimi Hendrix

The House of the Rising Sun by The Animals

Bed of Roses by Bon Jovi

Scar Tissue by Red Hot Chili Peppers

Just the Way You Are by Bruno Mar

HOW TO PLAY
GUITAR
IN 1 DAY
The Only 7 Exercises You Need to
Learn Guitar Chords, Guitar Scales
and Guitar Tabs Today
PRESTON HOFFMAN

BOOK 2

HOW TO PLAY GUITAR: IN 1 DAY

The Only 7 Exercises You Need to Learn Guitar Chords, Guitar Scales and Guitar Tabs Today

Preston Hoffman

Table of Contents

Introduction

Thank you for purchasing this book. You are now already on your way to becoming a guitarist.

The guitar is one of the most versatile instruments that there is and one of the most straightforward to play. Becoming a player opens you to a world of fun, relaxation and satisfaction.

For some, it might lead to a bit of extra income, if you join a band. Making music is a wonderful thing; making it in the company of others is even better.

By buying this book, you have made the first move to acquiring lifelong skills, which will provide much laughter, much joy and immense satisfaction.

We suggest that you work through this book a chapter at a time, spending long enough in each lesson to have secured the skills before moving on to the next chapter. It may seem hard at the outset, but it will quickly become easier.

This is a very practical book. You will be playing straight away. There are two useful chapters at the end, which offer more detail on questions that might arise, and a glossary of terms. There are also some songs to get you playing.

Mostly, this book will introduce you to playing the guitar. Give yourself a day, and you will be well on your way.

Chapter One: Getting Started – Lesson One - The Parts of the Guitar, and How to Hold It

The saying goes that there is no time like the present, so if your aim is to learn to play the guitar quickly, let us get straight into it.

Essential Information

A few notes, though, before we start. There is a glossary at the back of this book. Any term followed by an asterisk (*) will be defined in the alphabetical glossary at the end.

Secondly, a very useful tip is to get your head around each chapter before moving on to the next. The better understanding you have of each section, the more rapid your progress will be.

In addition, the learning will stick, and you will not have to constantly look back to re-learn the skills that this book will help you to acquire.

Next, don't worry if you get sore fingers on your left (fret*) hand, especially if you are playing a steel string guitar. The skin on the end of your fingers will quickly harden and the soreness will disappear.

OK, let's get on with it. For the purposes of the rest of the chapter, the assumption is made that you already have your guitar, and that it is stringed and tuned*. If not, there are sections on choosing your guitar, stringing it and tuning the instrument later in the book.

The Parts of the Guitar

The guitar is formed from a few basic parts, each of which has their individual role. It doesn't really matter which kind of guitar you own, because the make-up is the same. If you have an electric guitar, there will be extra knobs and levers, but we will look at these later.

Guitar Head and Tuning Pegs

The head has two primary purposes. It is there to help sustain, or lengthen, the sound of the strings.

If you put your hand on the head, and play the open* strings with the other hand, you will sense the vibrations of the notes continuing to make a sound.

The second role of the head is hold the tuning pegs. These are the pegs connected to the rollers around which the strings are held tight. Turning these pegs changes the note. See the section on 'tuning' for more details.

Heads look different on the various types of guitar; do not worry about this, as they all perform the same task.

Guitar Neck and Nut

The picture above shows the nut. This is the part of the that holds the strings in place.

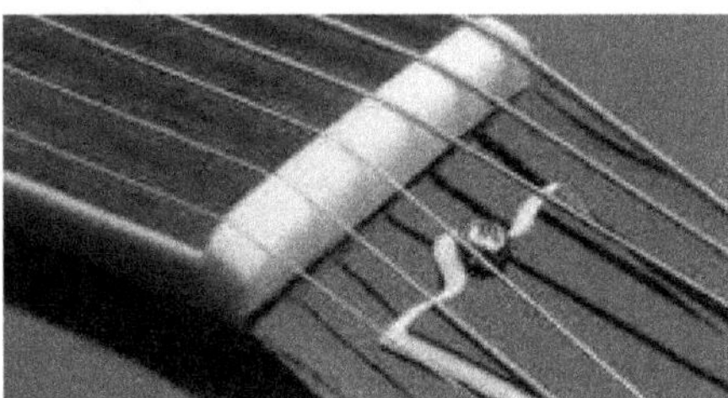

The nut has six little slots into each of which a string fits. It ensures that a full sound is heard by keeping the string away from the neck and frets.

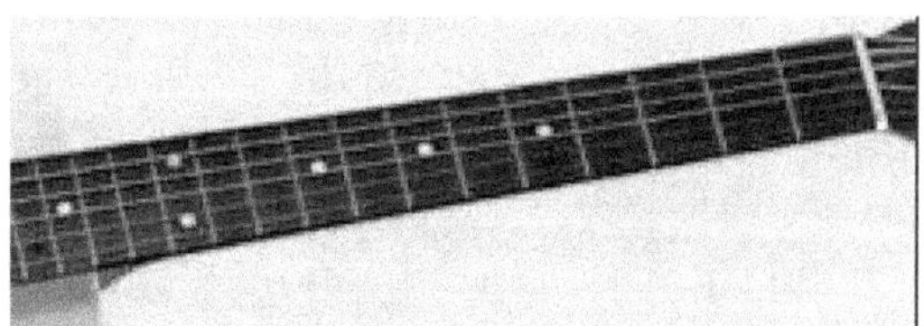

The picture above shows the neck of a guitar. This is the long section on which the frets are located. The example above has fret markers – the little dots that help the player to locate the appropriate fret when playing down the neck, which is more difficult than playing up at the head end. Not all guitars have these markers.

Here we can see the body of the guitar. The hole in the middle is called the sound hole, which is there to amplify the sound of the guitar. Electric guitars do not have these, as they have pick-ups (raised metal bars) to send the vibrations electronically to the amplifier.

Note that the body shape of a guitar can take many forms, especially with electric guitars. The final part of the guitar to identify is the bridge, into which the ends of the strings are fitted.

Holding the Guitar

As a beginner, it is best to start with a sitting position. As players become more experienced, then it is possible to play standing up, but the extra support offered when sitting helps the new player.

The position above is the classical stance when playing the Spanish* guitar. Note that the left foot is raised. A footrest can be purchased to facilitate this, but a pile of books or a block of wood works just as well. The guitar sits on the left leg, with the right just offering support. Both hands then fit into the natural position.

For larger guitars, such as acoustics*, then the picture below offers a more usual position. Here, the guitar is on the right leg, with the two legs close together. Of the two, the better one for the beginner is the Spanish guitar position. However, comfort is the most important thing of all.

Chapter Summary

So now we have the basics.

- You know the names of the parts of the guitar
- You know how to hold the instrument

In the next chapter you will begin to learn how to play.

Chapter Two: Lesson Two - Chords

In this chapter we will learn about the basic chords* which will allow you to begin to play songs almost immediately.

For a right-handed person, or somebody who plays right handed (most people do…) chords are formed with the left hand. Many songs can be played with just a collection of three or four chords, and in this chapter, we will look at the main ones.

There are seven notes in music, and chords are named after these. Chords are MAJOR* chords unless otherwise stated. Major chords make a kind of complete sound, whereas the other main form, MINOR* chords, make a sort of questioning, unfinished sound. Once you play one of each, the difference will be clear.

There are numerous varieties after that, but for this book, as it is for beginners, we will stick to just one alternative, a 7th chord*. This is a chord with an extra note (a seventh above the base note, for those interested).

The chords below are the ones that appear most commonly. Some, such as for example, the B Major chord (B) will appear in later chapters because they require a barre to play.

A Chords

Here, the lowest E string is not strummed*, the other five strings are. Use your first finger to cover the four strings on the second fret, then press the bottom string with your little finger

A

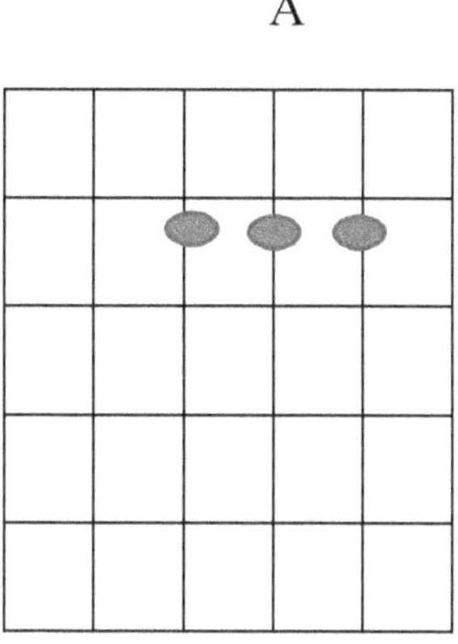

Am (A minor)

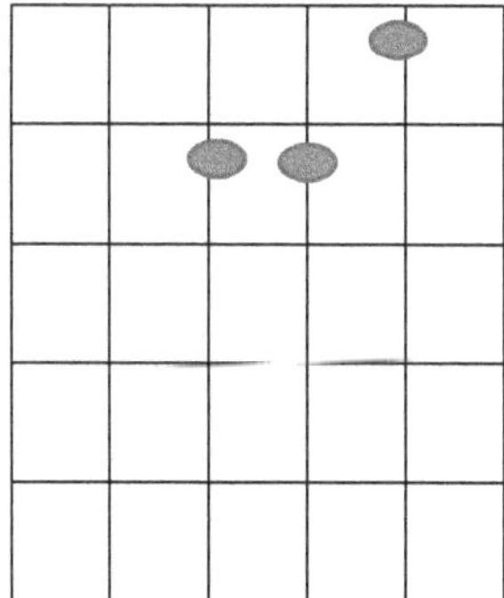

A7

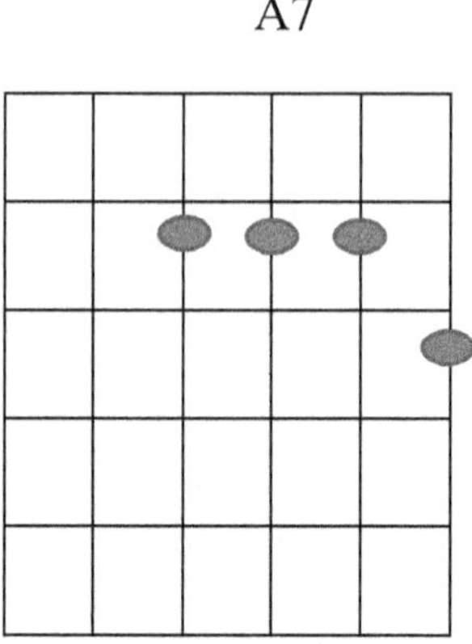

Use your first finger to cover the four strings on the second fret, then press the bottom string with your little finger

Am7

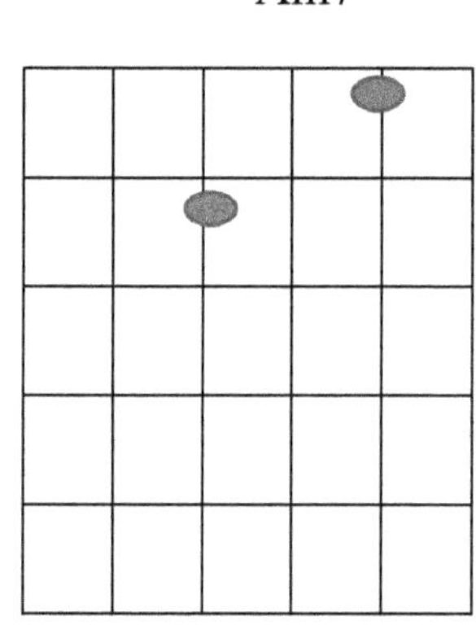

C Chords

As with A chords, the lowest E string is not strummed.

C

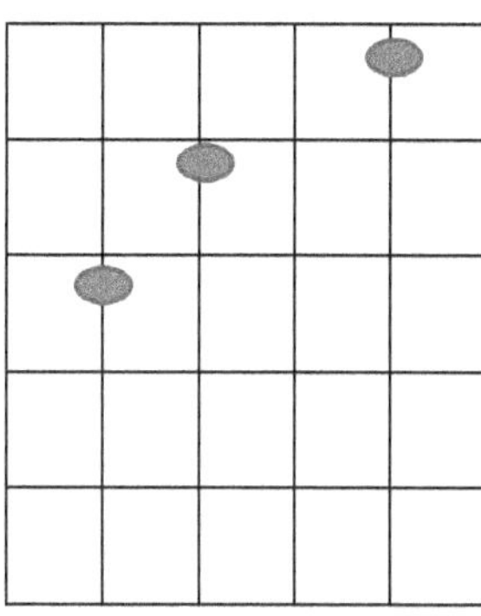

C7

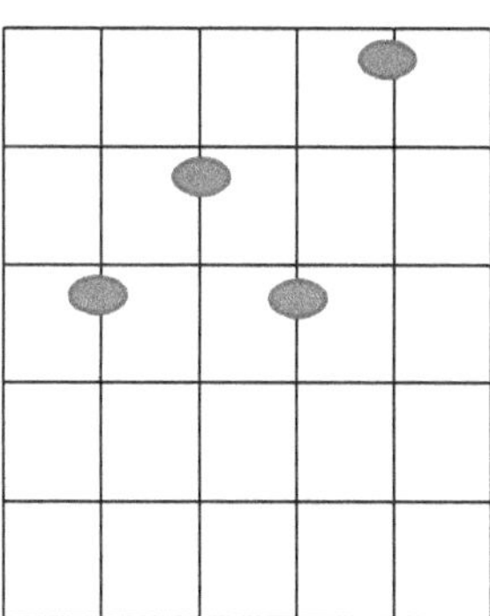

D Chords

Here, the lowest two strings, E and A, are not strummed.

D

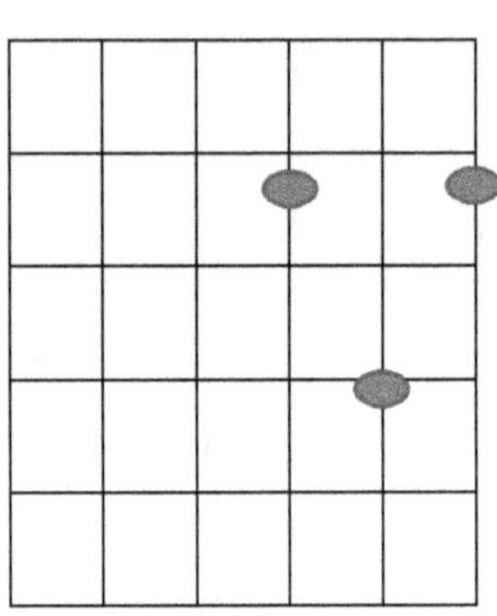

Dm

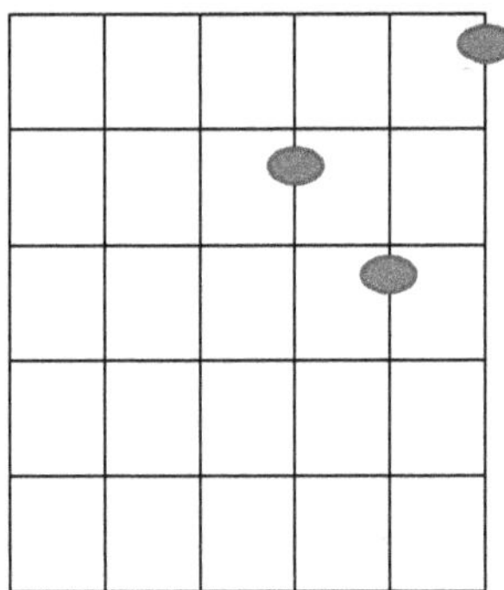

D7

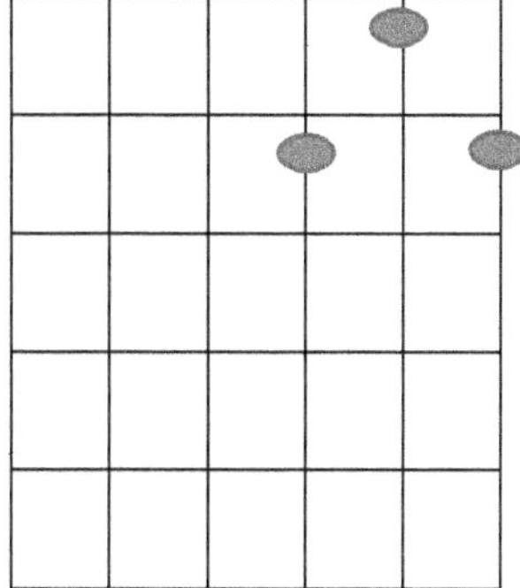

Dm7

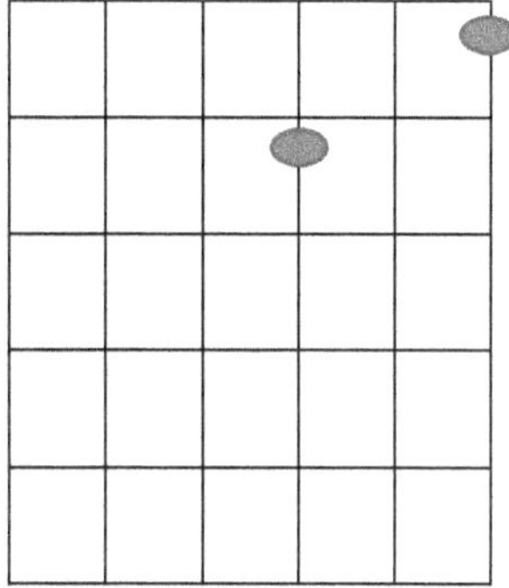

E Chords

Here, all strings are strummed.

E

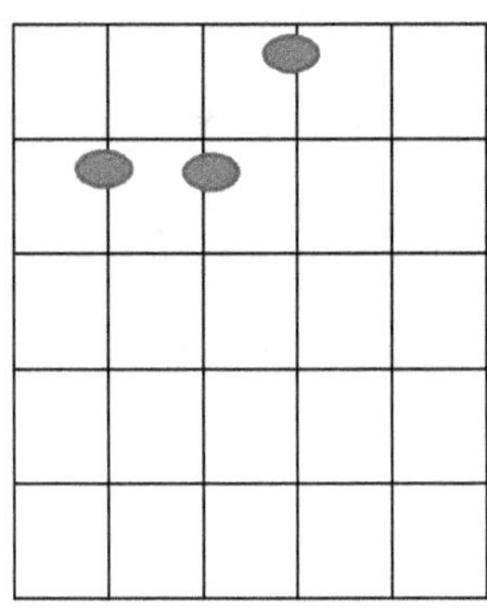

Em

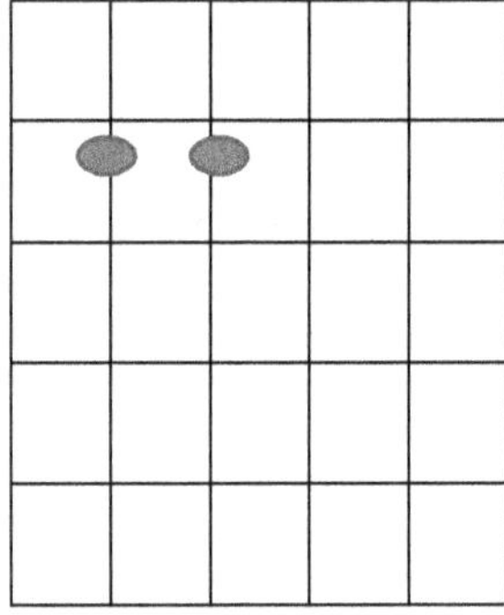

E7

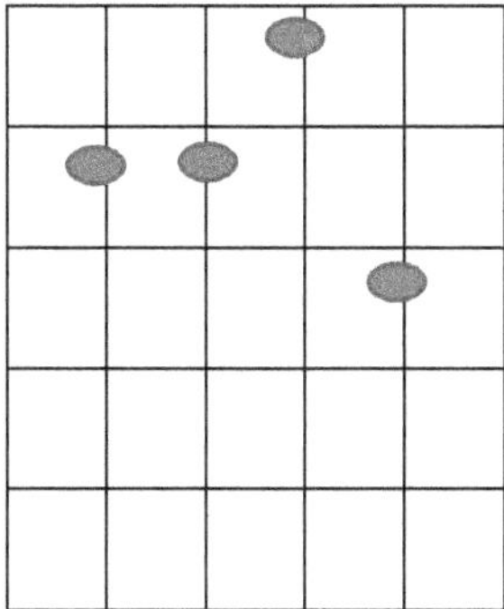

Use your first finger to cover the four strings on the second fret, then press the bottom string with your little finger

Em7

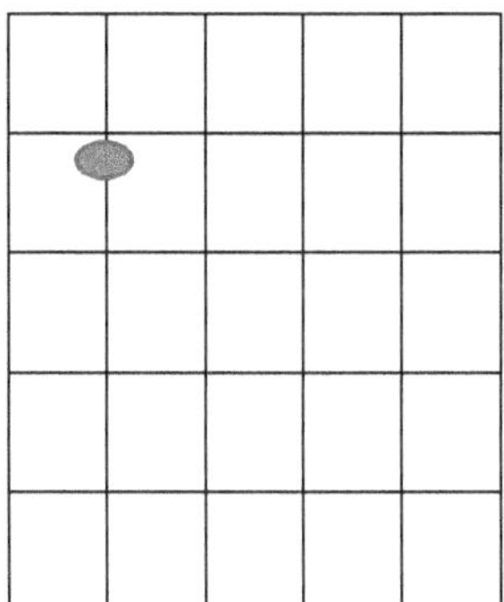

F Chords

If a barre is used, all strings are strummed, if not then the E and A strings are not strummed.

F

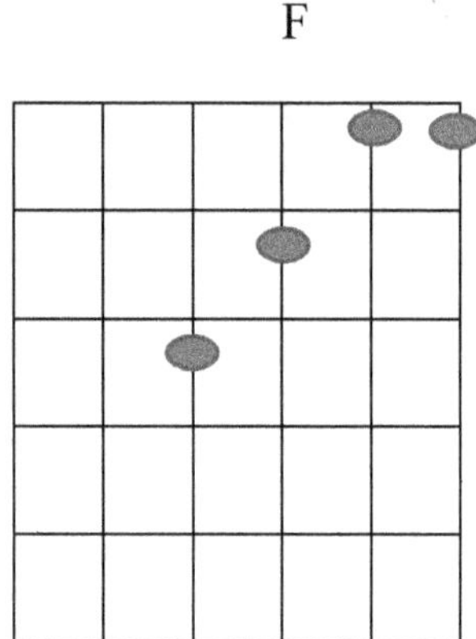

Use your first finger to hold down the first two strings. If you can, the first finger can create a bar by stretching over all six strings. It takes a bit of strength, but that soon develops.

G Chords

All strings are strummed.

G

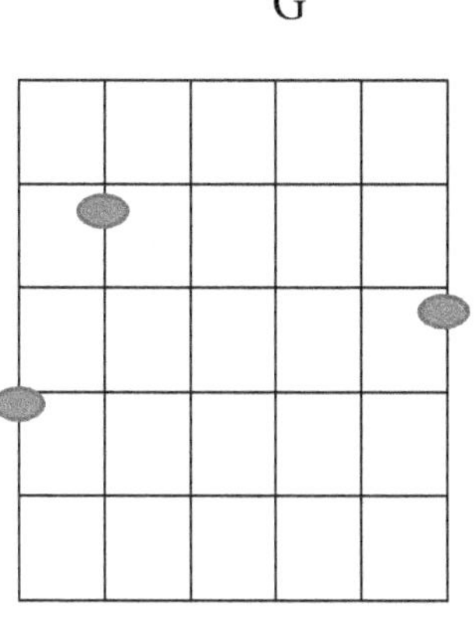

G7

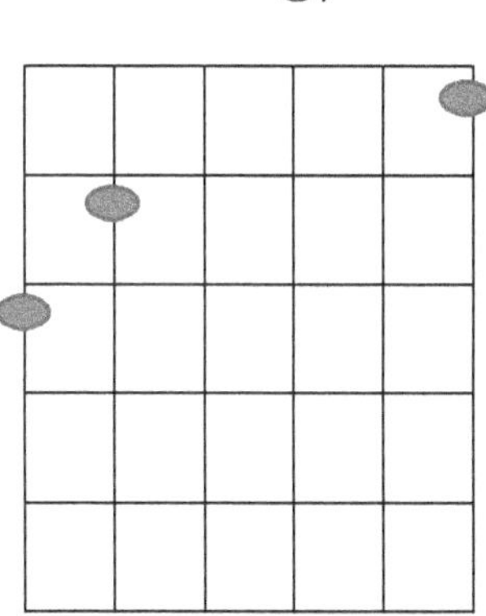

The key with these chords is to practice them. Get them so that you can form each chord and play them so that there is no buzzing of the strings, or 'flat' sounds of a string not being pushed down firmly enough.

Progressions

Songs are often built around chord progressions. These are chords that simply go together well. Practice these and you will be able to use them in a wide range of songs.

The Most Common Progression

This works in any key, but for our purposes we will practice C, F and G

C C C C F F F F G G G G C C C C

Songs such as John Lennon's Imagine follow this progression.

Pop Progressions

These chord combinations work in popular songs such as Someone Like You by Adele. The chords are C, G, Am and F.

C C C C G G G G Am Am Am Am F F F F C C C C etc

Jazz Progressions

Everything from Boyfriend, the Justin Bieber, ummm, song and some of Queen's Bohemian Rhapsody follow this progression, which features the chords Dm, G and C.

Dm Dm Dm Dm G G G G C C C C Dm Dm Dm Dm etc

The Progression from the Fifties

Common in fact from the 1940s to the 1960s for both ballads and more upbeat songs, there are two progressions here. Firstly, is C Am Dm and G and songs such as the Beatles' The Fool on the Hill used this.

C C C C Am Am Am Am Dm Dm Dm Dm G G G G C C C C

Similar to this is the second progression which was used by the late great Leonard Cohen in the much-recorded Hallelujah. Here, the chords of C Am F and G are used.

C C C C Am Am Am Am F F F F G G G G

Chapter Summary

In this Chapter, we have presented all the most common chords that do not require a barre.

- o These chords come in the major form, which is usually known just by its letter, that is, C is the same as C major
- o They come in a seventh form
- o The can also come in a minor form as well as a minor seventh version
- o Chords are often put together in what are called progressions, and which form the basis of many songs.

In the next chapter you will learn a little bit about strumming.

Chapter Three: Lesson Three - Strumming

Before reading any further, give yourself a bit of a treat. Put your favourite CD, record, iPod song or whatever on to play. Listen carefully to the rhythm and count the beats of the drum. Sometimes, you can hear this on the guitars as well, but the drum is usually clearest.

What you are listening to is the beat of the song, sometimes called the time signature. In other words, the number of beats in a bar of music. If you learn to read music, this will be very important to help you play, but for the moment, just understanding about different rhythms in the simplest form is all that is needed.

Tap along to the beat, get that rhythm in your bones. What you will notice is that most, but not all, songs are written in 4/4 timing, that means that there are four beats in the bar. They might be played as eight quick beats, or two heavy and two light ones, or just 1,2,3,4; by counting or tapping your foot along you will see that the song is divided into blocks of four.

There are other rhythms, 3/4 is the beat of the waltz – **dum**, dee, dee, **dum**, dee, dee, **dum**, dee, dee, **dum**, dee, dee, etc. But we will start with four beats to the bar.

One tool here that can be very useful is a metronome, which is a device which ticks a steady rhythm out. You can buy a modern digital one from about $16, or a traditional one with a lever for about $100, which also makes a great ornament.

Or, there are apps available for your phone and free online versions. What the metronome will do, as it clicks away at the speed you set, is to help you keep a constant beat. This is really important as the guitar frequently supplies the rhythm for a song.

Basic Four-Four Rhythms

For each of the following, start by using you thumb, then add in a forefinger if it feels comfortable, finally, try it with a plectrum*.

Hold a chord that you feel comfortable making, and when you get the feel change the chord after ever bar, or four beats.

Set the metronome to sixty beats per minute, then when you get the hang of the rhythm, increase it to eighty beats per minute.

Example One

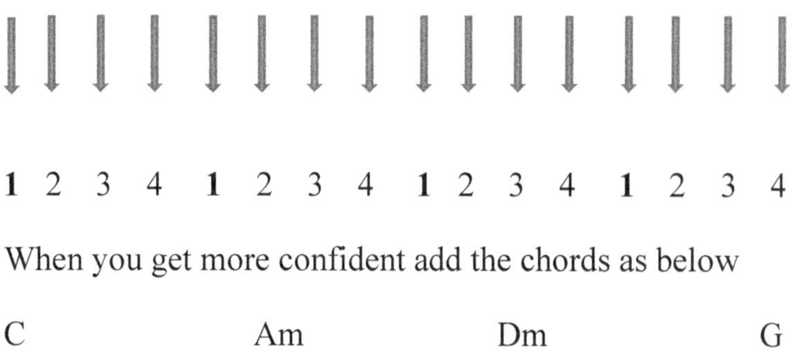

1 2 3 4   1 2 3 4   1 2 3 4   1 2 3 4

When you get more confident add the chords as below

C   Am   Dm   G

Example Two

This time you will strum twice as quickly, getting eight strokes in each four beats. Start with a down beat / strum and follow it with an upbeat. Once again, add the different chords when you have the hang of it. Don't forget to use your metronome to make sure you maintain a rhythm and keep time.

Example Three

Once you have these basics, then we can go for something very complicated. After you have mastered this and the chords we have shown you, you really will be able to call yourself a guitar player. Perhaps not yet an Eric Clapton, Jimi Hendrix or Paul

Simon, but definitely someone who can bash out a beat, play the chords and make it sound good.

As before, start with the single chord and the slow speed, then build things up. Note the direction of the strokes.

Note that here the first 'stroke' of the third beat does not happen. The effect you are looking to achieve is **DUM   DEE DEE pause DEE DEE DEE DUM   DEE DEE pause DEE DEE DEE** etc.

A Tip for the Plectrum

It is best to start with a medium weight plectrum, as they are easiest to manipulate. Heavy ones can get caught on the strings, and lightweight ones can be harder to control. Hold the plectrum between your thumb and first finger, and curl the other fingers up into a loose fist. Hold the plectrum towards the top, so just over half is exposed to strike the strings. You do not want the strings to catch on your fingers.

Finally, remember when strumming that the movement comes from the wrist, not the whole arm. The great arm flashing helicopter rotors of Pete Townshend and other performers are for show, not effect. Just a small rotation of the wrist leads to controlled, pure strumming with a great sound.

Chapter Summary

In this chapter we have learned a little about strumming, the technique and some rhythms that can be played.

In the next chapter we will learn something a little more technical: reading tabs.

Chapter Four: Lesson Four - Reading Tabs

There are four basic ways to play the notes and chords, found in a piece of music, on the guitar. These are:

- Reading the Music
- Playing by Ear
- Reading Chord Names
- Playing by Tab

Reading Music

The guitar is unusual when it comes to instruments. First, compared to most, it is relatively easy to learn. There is none of the complex finger movements of the piano, breathing challenges of wind and brass instruments or judgement of tone and pitch associated with the likes of the violin and cello.

That means that players are often self-taught, from books such as this, or have picked it up from friends. Learning to read music is a very useful skill indeed, but it is time consuming and needs a lot of practice. It tends to be an element left out when learning the guitar without the benefit of formal tutorage.

However, there is a use in knowing where the various notes are located on the guitar. These are presented in the table below. Along the top are the fret positions, down the side are the strings to which the fret position is related and finally in the middle is the note played. The logical pattern will quickly become apparent. Remember that the following pairs of notes are the same:

A# and Bb, C# and Db, D# and Eb, F# and Gb, G# and Ab

Open	First	Second	Third	Fourth	Fifth	Sixth	Seventh	Eighth
E (first)	F	F#	G	G#	A	Bb	B	C
B (second)	C	C#	D	Eb	E	F	F#	G
G (third)	G#	A	Bb	B	C	C#	D	Eb
D (fourth)	Eb	E	F	F#	G	G#	A	Bb
A (fifth)	Bb	B	C	C#	D	Eb	E	F
E (sixth)	F	F#	G	G#	A	Bb	B	C

Playing by Ear

There are some natural musicians who can just hear a piece, and know how to play it and which chords or notes to use. Sadly, not many of us fit into that category.

Playing by Chords

This is the easiest way of playing. Here, the chords to play are written above the lyrics of the song. The only problem is that if you do not know the song, it can be very hard to play. Getting the placement of the actual chord changes is also very difficult. Simply placing the fingers in the exact place is a challenge. There are some songs using this method later in the book, to get players started.

Playing by Tab

This might seem complicated at first, but with a bit of time, can be a very helpful way of overcoming the difficulties listed above.

The tab is a horizontal box with six lines, each one equating to one of the guitar's strings. The lowest represents the low E string, next is the A string, the D string, G string, then one from the top is the B string, with the top line equating to the higher pitched E string.

Numbers printed on the strings relate to the fret that the string should be played on. A '0' means that the string should be played open.

Chords are a little more complicated, but still quick to learn. Here, numbers appear on all the strings.

Can you work out which chord the following tablature represents?

It is, of course, E major. Strings 1 (E), 2 (B) and 6 (E) are open, then the G string is played on the first fret, and strings 4 and 5, (D and A) are played on the second fret.

To help even more, tablature, or tabs, will usually feature the chord's name as well.

A little later we will learn a bit about finger picking. This is when the notes of the chord are played individually by the fingers of, for right handed players, the right hand. The proper name for this is an arpeggiated chord*.

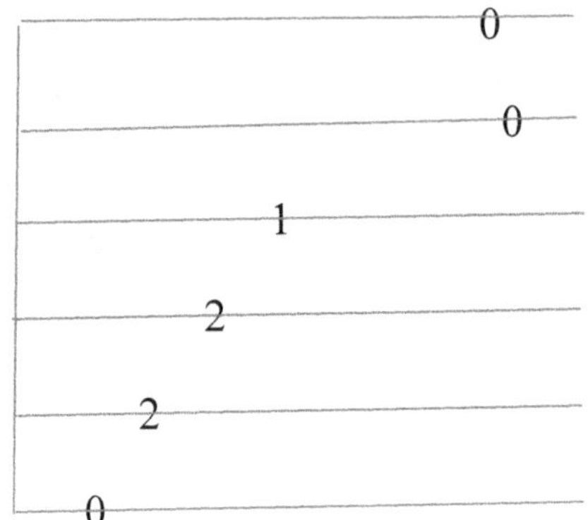

The arpeggiated E major chord will look like the diagram above.

Where a string should not be played, it is indicated by an X. There are numerous other signs in tablature, which can be investigated when a player is more competent with their instrument, but this is enough information for the first stages of playing, especially as this book aims to get players up and running, at the most basic level, within a day.

Chapter Summary

In this chapter we have learned four ways of playing the guitar. By chord, by ear, by music and by tab.

- o Playing by chord is the most straightforward, but is a rough science.

- o   Tab and music are accurate, but trickier (especially by music).
- o   Playing by ear is an aptitude all musicians would like, but few possess.

In the next chapter we talk about barre chords, the method by which any chord can be played.

Chapter Five: Lesson Five - Barre Chords

In this chapter you will learn about how the barre can turn the basic chord shapes into any chord.

Creating the barre can be tiring at first, and strength needs to build up in the hand. It is easiest on an electric guitar, where the neck is slim and the strings are usually lightweight. The Spanish guitar is hardest because of the width of the neck and the bulkiness of the strings.

Below we can see how the basic E chord fingering turns into the chord of F when it is shifted down a fret, and the index finger makes a barre behind it.

Here are some of the chords that we did not show earlier, with their barre in place

F

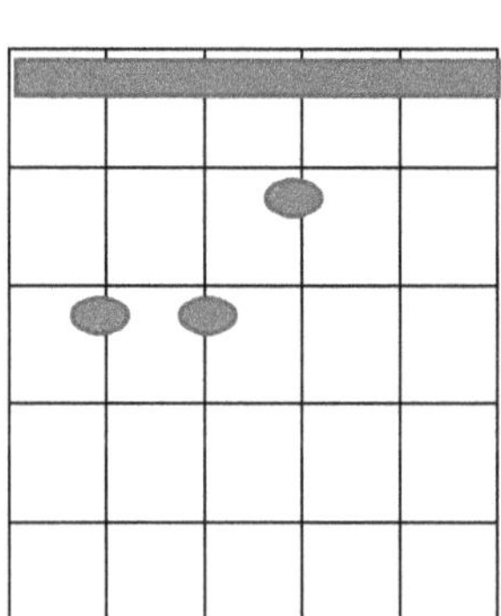

B Chords

B

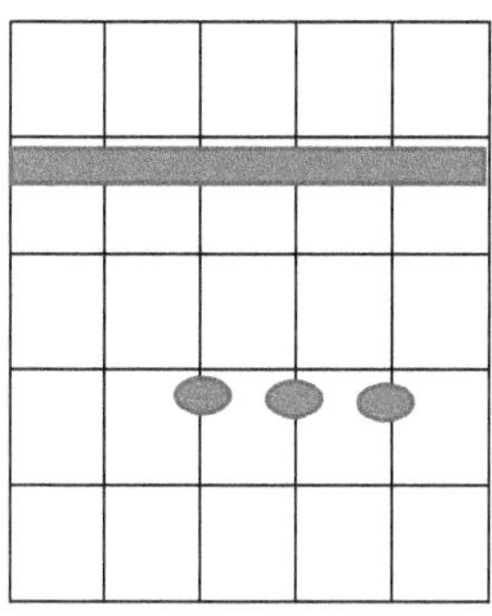

Bm

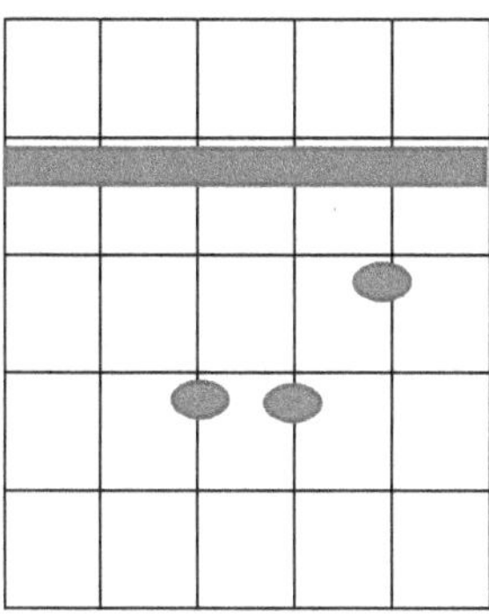

B7 (no low E strummed)

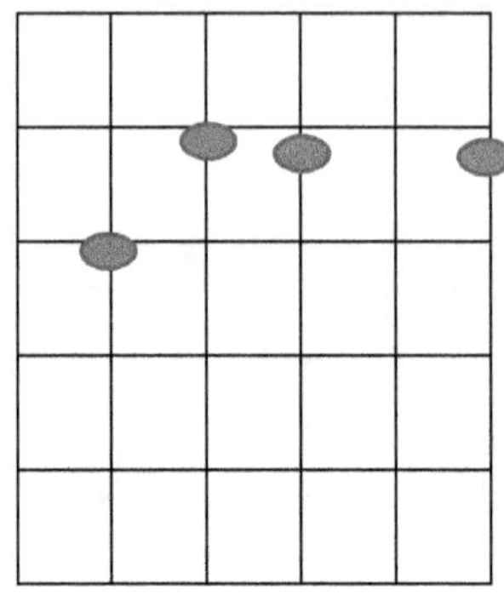

Bm7

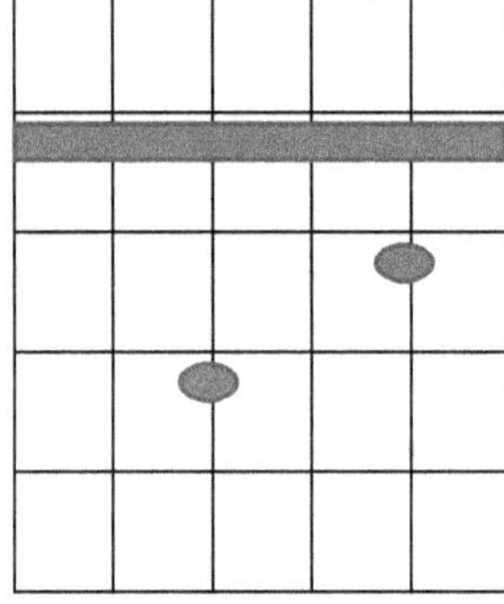

F Chords

Fm

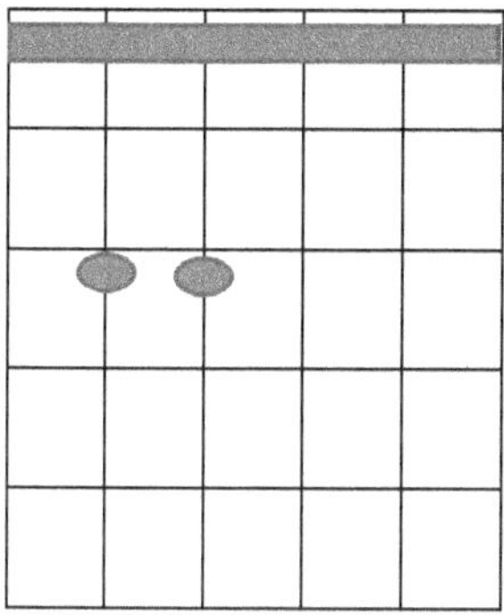

F7

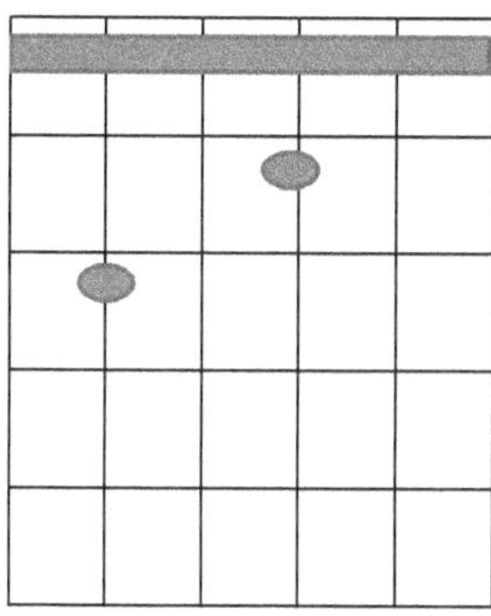

Fm7

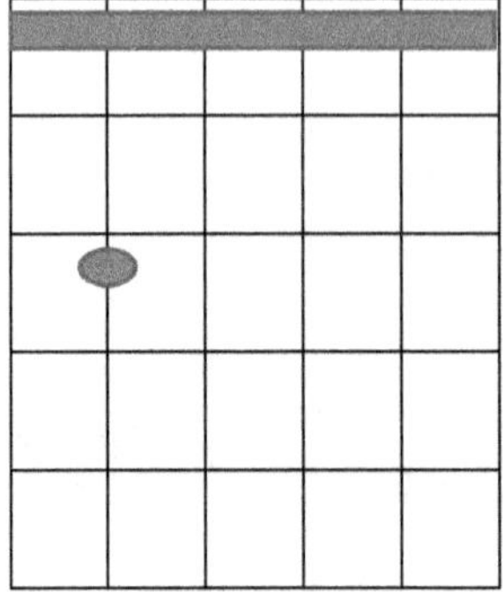

G Chords

Gm

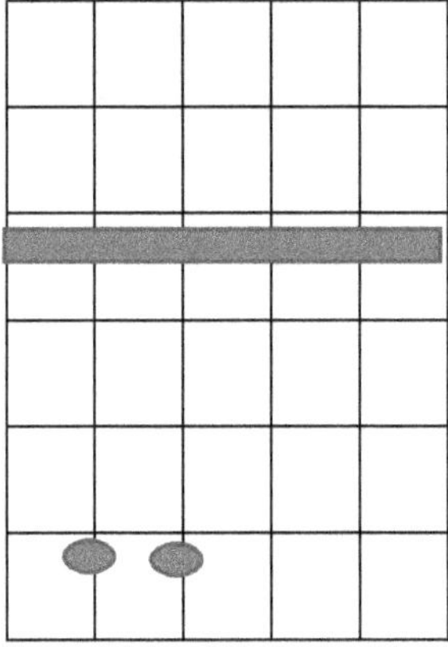

Gm7

Sharps and Flats

Sharp and flat chords tend to be made using a barre. The most common chords here are F sharp (F#), C#, B flat (Bb) and Eb, although there are several more.

F#

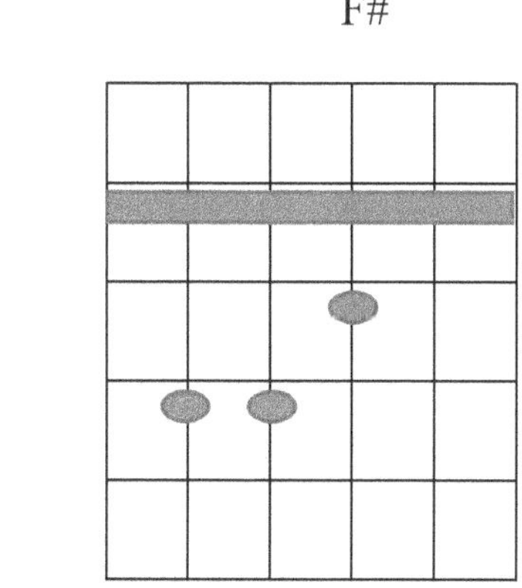

C#

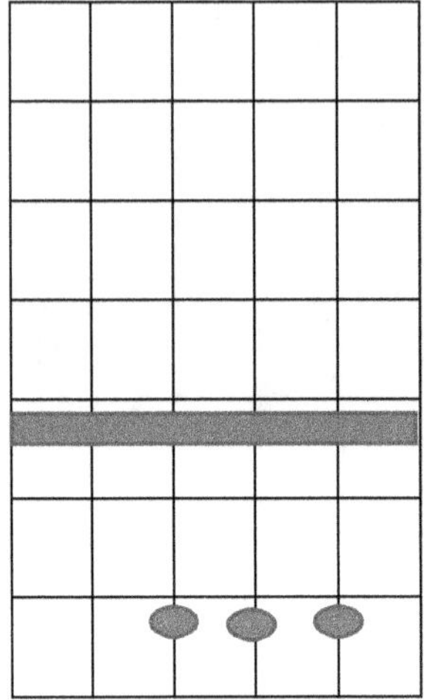

Bb

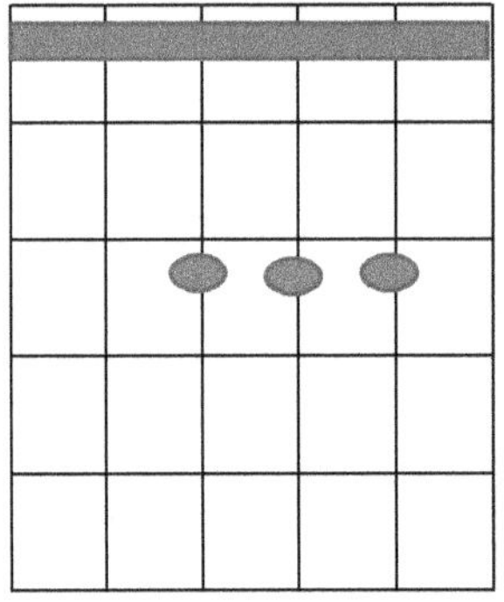

Eb

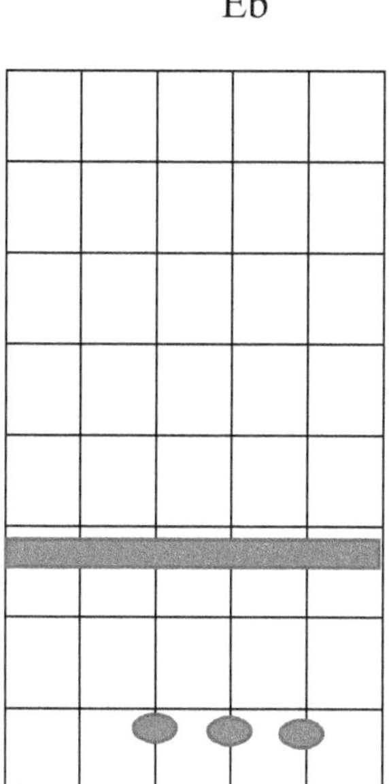

As many of you will have spotted, it is possible to play the same chord in many ways using a barre. This can make chord changes easier as players become more experienced. Although the chord is the same, the pitch and quality of sound will vary depending on where on the fretboard* the chord is played.

Chord Table

The table below shows how various chords are formed depending on where they are played on the fretboard. Chord shapes are listed across the top, and the fret on which the barre is held down the side.

In the middle is the chord that is formed. The pattern can be repeated for any cord shape, although these are the shapes that are usually to be found used with a barre.

		E	Em	Em7	A	Am	Am7
1st		F	Fm	Fm7	Bb	Bbm	Bbm7
2nd		F#	F#m	F#m7	B	Bm	Bm7
3rd		G	Gm	Gm7	C	Cm	Cm7
4th		Ab	G#m	G#m7	C#	C#m	C#m7
5th		A	Am	Am7	D	Dm	Dm7
6th		Bb	Bbm	Bbm7	Eb	Ebm	Ebm7
7th		B	Bm	Bm7	E	Em	Em7
8th		C	Cm	Cm7	F	Fm	Fm7

Chapter Summary

In this chapter we have looked at the barre.

- We have seen that the barre accompanied by the shapes of other chords can create new chords.

- Practising with a barre makes chord changes easier.

In the next chapter you will learn more about those essentials of instrument playing, scales.

Chapter Six: Lesson Six - Guitar Scales

Quite a short chapter this one, but a very important one. Scales are the notes that are contained within a particular key in music. Songs are written in keys, and by knowing the notes that are involved in that key, it is possible to play accompaniments and lead guitar to go with it.

A great way to warm up is to run through a couple of scales, it gets the fingers of both hands working, and over time the notes will become engrained in your head. You will then know, even if you are just reading the chords involved in a piece, the key in which it is based.

The tables below show the notes involved in all the major and minor keys. The numbers on the left indicate the place of that note in the scale, while the keys are across the top.

Major Keys

	A	Bb	B	C	Db	D	Eb	E	F	F#	G	Ab
1	A	Bb	B	C	Db	D	Eb	E	F	F#	G	Ab
2	B	C	Db	D	Eb	E	F	F#	G	G#	A	Bb
3	C#	D	Eb	E	F	F#	G	G#	A	Bb	B	C
4	D	Eb	E	F	F#	G	Ab	A	Bb	B	C	Db
5	E	F	F#	G	Ab	A	Bb	B	C	C#	D	Eb
6	F#	G	Ab	A	Bb	B	C	C#	D	D#	E	F
7	Ab	A	Bb	B	C	C#	D	D#	E	F	F#	G
8	A	Bb	B	C	Db	D	Eb	E	F	F#	G	Ab

Minor Keys (Harmonic Minors)

	A m	Bb m	B m	C m	C# m	D m	Eb m	E m	F m	F# m	G m	G# m
1	A	Bb	B	C	C#	D	Eb	E	F	F#	G	G#
2	B	C	C	D	D#	E	F	F#	G	G#	A	A
3	C	Db	D	Eb	E	F	Gb	G	Ab	A	Bb	B
4	D	Eb	E	f	F#	G	Ab	A	Bb	B	C	C#
5	E	F	F#	G	G#	A	Bb	B	C	C#	D	D#
6	F	Gb	G	Ab	A	Bb	C	C	Db	D	E	E
7	G#	A	Bb	B	C	C#	D	D#	E	F	F#	G
8	A	Bb	B	C	C#	D	Eb	E	F	F#	G	G#

There are many different types of minor scales, such as harmonic (which is printed), melodic and natural scales. However, the harmonic is fine for using at the level we are currently at.

One of the most common and popular scales for the guitar is the blues scale.

The blues scale in C includes the following notes:

C	Eb	F	Gb	G	Bb	C

In the key of D, it looks like this:

D	F	G	Ab	A	C	D

Finally, we will learn the classic series of notes that, once mastered, lead to the classic 12 bar blues themes that underpin so many songs.

In tab form, it looks like this:

In notes, it is played as follows:

⬆	A	C	D	E	G	A	C	D	E	G	A	C	⬇
A	G	E	D	C	A	G	E	D	C	A			

Chapter Summary

Chapter six has introduced you to the concept of the musical scale. You have been given the notes involved in the different key signatures in which music is written.

In the next chapter you will learn more about plectrums or picks, and a little about finger picking.

Chapter Seven: Lesson Seven - Using a Plectrum and Finger Picking

As we saw earlier, there are many different weights of plectrum. It is best to start strumming with a middle weight one, and over time players will find the weight that suits them best, and which works for the kind of music they are playing. Heavy plectrums tend to be easier for picking notes if, for example, a combination of picking and strumming is required. Lightweight plectrums are handy for faster, smoother strumming. They are handy for electric guitars, where the sound is created electronically.

There are also thumb and finger picks which can be worn when picking notes. They can be tricky to use, catching on the strings, and a light action is needed. As a beginner, it is probably best to start picking using the fingers, rather than the picks shown below, but it is a matter of choice. A sharper sound is created with the picks.

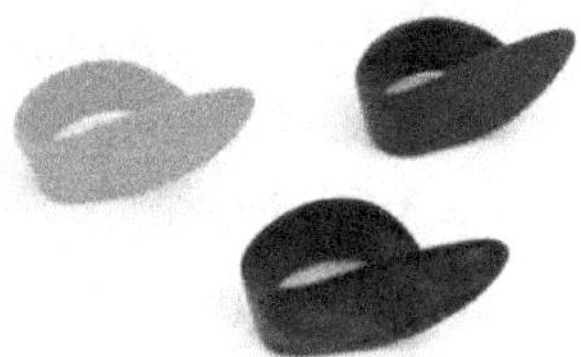

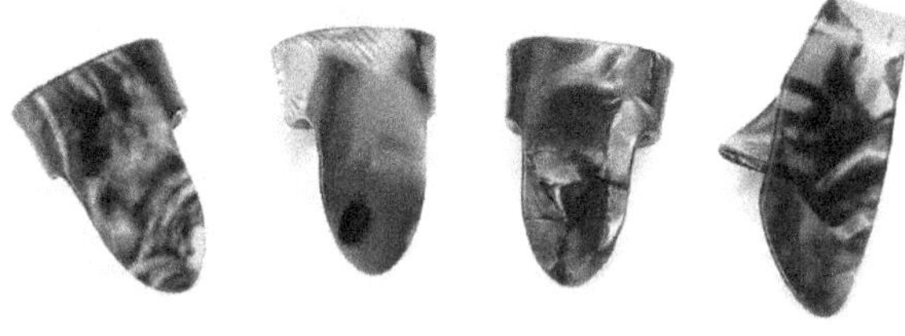

Whether picking or strumming, a different tone is created depending on where the action takes place. Playing over the sound hole (or pick up, with an electric guitar) creates the fullest, and loudest sound.

Move towards the bridge, and a harsher tone is produced. Unsurprisingly, playing closer to the neck makes for a softer, more mellifluous sound.

Finger Picking

Sometimes called finger style*, or plucking*, this is the method by which individual notes of a chord are played one after the other, often quite quickly. It is a style often associated with folk style music, and ballads.

Listen to Paul Simon playing the opening to the Simon and Garfunkel hit, The Boxer, to hear finger picking at its best.

Picking usually works as follows. The thumb plays any notes on the low E, A and D strings, while the first, second and third fingers pick notes from the G, B and E strings. Normally, the index finger will pluck the lowest string being played, usually the G string, with the middle finger next, usually the B string and the third finger used for the top E string. The little finger is not used, and many players place it under the sound hole on the body of the guitar to provide support and help the other fingers to remain in the correct place. The only time it would come into play is if there is a need to pluck five strings simultaneously.

Picking can be used with arpeggiated chords, and for playing pairs of notes together

An advantage of finger picking is that it turns the guitar into more than a percussive rhythm keeper. It allows for melodies to be interspersed with chords, and for the playing of harmonies (notes combined to produce a pleasing effect). Hammers* and pull offs* can also be incorporated into playing, as the guitarist becomes more competent. Tapping the body of the guitar to create a percussion effect is also easier than when working with a plectrum.

It is still possible to strum, using the thumb or first finger, but the sound created has a different quality to that created with a pick, and therefore it is not suitable for more upbeat rockier numbers.

Finger pickers need to keep their hands in good condition. The right hand always needs short finger nails for pressing the strings, and the same is true for the finger picker, unless they choose to use artificial picks. A nail too long will catch on the string, spoiling the effect being sought.

Another advantage with finger picking is that a greater variety of sound can be created. Generally, the volume will be lower, but varying the position of where the strings are plucked, and the force with which this happens, can alter the timbre*, to create mood and atmosphere in a song.

More flexibility is offered when playing, flamenco style strumming, plucking of multiple strings, arpeggios and such like all are easier to play with fingerpicking. However, the strings used should be nylon or light gauge steel, unless an artificial pick is attached to the fingers, to prevent nail and finger damage.

All the above makes it clear that finger picking lends itself to classical, solo guitar playing or playing as an accompaniment to voice or just perhaps one or two other instruments.

When finger picking is notarised in a piece of music, it will usually adopt the following notations:

Thumb = B

Index = I

Middle = M

Ring = A

Little = C or X or E

What's Next

As with everything else when learning the guitar, practice is all.

There are two simple finger picking exercises that can be practised to get the player into the swing.

For each, use the thumb for the E, A and D strings, the index finger for the G string, middle finger for the B string and third finger for the top E.

Use the chord progressions from earlier to practice. Set the metronome for 60 – it can get faster as you progress.

The first pattern is for 3/4 timing, the second for 4/4.

We will use the Dm, C, G, Dm progression in the example below. We will be playing two strings for each beat of the bar.

It goes something like this:

3/4 Example

The top row represents the chord, the second the finger playing and the third is the beat.

Dm						C						G						Dm					
T	I	M	A	M	I	T	I	M	A	M	I	T	I	M	A	M	I	T	I	M	A	M	I
1		2		3		1		2		3		1		2		3		1		2		3	

And so on…

4/4 Example

Dm								C								G							
T	I	M	A	M	I	T	I	T	I	M	A	M	I	T	I	T	I	M	A	M	I	T	I
1		2		3		4		1		2		3		4		1		2		3		4	

Chapter Summary

In this chapter we have learned a bit about finger picking, its uses and tools that can help.

- We know about how the notation is present
- We have undertaken some practice
- We know the kind of music with which it works best.

In the next chapter we will present some songs for you to play.

Chapter Eight: Some Songs To Play

Below are some songs along with their chords. They are well known, and if one is unfamiliar, they can be found easily on the internet. For legal reasons, we can only print songs that are out of copywrite, but there are hundreds of examples of popular music on the internet, plus countless books available from your local music stores.

Sing along with the songs, it will help you to 'feel' where the changes take place and keep you in time.

Happy Birthday

```
  A      E
Happy Birthday to you
  D    A
Happy Birthday to you
  A7       D
Happy Birthday dear Billy (please feel free to substitute a
name!)
  A   E   A
Happy Birthday to you.
```

Morning Has Broken

```
        C  Dm  G           F   C
Morning has broken, like the first morning
(C)         Em  Am  D7      D   G
Blackbird has spoken, like the first bird
C         F    C          Am   D
Praise for the singing, praise for the morning
G           C  F  G7        C    F
Praise for the springing fresh from the world
[Interlude]
G  E  Am  G  C  G7
            C  Dm    G         F   C
Sweet the rain's new fall, sunlit from heaven
(C)         Em  Am  D7      D   G
Like the first dewfall, on the first grass
C          F    C        Am   D
Praise for the sweetness of the wet garden
G          C  F  G7        C    F
Sprung in completeness where his feet pass
[Interlude]
G  E  Am  F#  Bm  G  D  A7/D  D
        D  Em   A         G   D
Mine is the sunlight, mine is the morning
        F#m Bm    E7       A
Born of the one light, Eden saw play
D        G   D          Bm  E
Praise with elation, praise every morning
A        D G  A7       D
```

God's recreation of the new day

G A F# Bm   G7   C   F   C

      C Dm G   F   C
Morning has broken, like the first morning
(C)   Em Am D7   D   G
Blackbird has spoken, like the first bird
C   F   C   Am   D
Praise for the singing, praise for the morning
G   C F G7   C   F
Praise for the springing fresh from the world
[Outro]
G E Am F# Bm G D A7/D D

She'll Be Coming Round the Mountain

G
She'll be coming 'round the mountain
    G
When she comes.
    G
She'll be coming 'round the mountain
    D7
When she comes.
    G
She'll be coming 'round the mountain,
    C
She'll be coming 'round the mountain,
    G   D7
She'll be coming 'round the mountain,
    G
When she comes.

[Verse 2]
    G
She'll be driving six white horses
    G
When she comes
    G
She'll be driving six white horses
    D7
When she comes

                G
She'll be driving six white horses
                C
She'll be driving six white horses
              G   D7
She'll be driving six white horses
        G
When she comes

[Verse 3]
        G
Oh, we'll all come out to meet her
        G
When she comes
        G
Oh, we'll all come out to meet her
        D7
When she comes
        G
Oh, we'll all come out to meet her
        C
Oh, we'll all come out to meet her
        G   D7
Oh, we'll all come out to meet her
        G
When she comes

[Verse 4]
        G
We will kill the old red rooster
        G

When she comes
     G
We will kill the old red rooster
      D7
When she comes
     G
We will kill the old red rooster
     C
We will kill the old red rooster
     G   D7
We will kill the old red rooster
      G
When she comes

[Verse 5]
    G
We'll all have chicken n' dumplin's
       G
When she comes
    G
We'll all have chicken n' dumplin's
      D7
When she comes
    G
We'll all have chicken n' dumplin's
     C
We'll all have chicken n' dumplin's
     G   D7
We'll all have chicken n' dumplin's
      G

When she comes

Swing Low, Sweet Chariot

```
C
I looked over Jordan,
  F        C
And what did I see,
                 G7
Comin' for to carry me home,
  C          F          C
A band of angels comin' after me,
        G7      C
Comin' for to carry me home.


        C        F   C
Swing Low, sweet chariot,
                 G7
Comin' for to carry me home;
        C      F   C
Swing low, sweet chariot,
C          G7      C
Comin' for to carry me home.
```

The Drunken Sailor

Em
What shall we do with the drunken sailor?
D
What shall we do with the drunken sailor?
Em
What shall we do with the drunken sailor?

[Chorus]

Em D   Em
Ear-ly in the morning
Em
Hooray, and up she rises
D
Hooray, and up she rises
Em
Hooray, and up she rises
Em D   Em
Ear-ly in the morning

[Verse]

Em
Put him in the long boat 'til he's sober
D

Put him in the long boat 'til he's sober
Em
Put him in the long boat 'til he's sober

[Chorus]

Em D   Em
Ear-ly in the morning
Em
Hooray, and up she rises
D
Hooray, and up she rises
Em
Hooray, and up she rises
Em D   Em
Ear-ly in the morning

[Verse]

Em
Pull out the plug and wet him all over
D
Pull out the plug and wet him all over
Em
Pull out the plug and wet him all over

[Chorus]

Em D   Em
Ear-ly in the morning
Em
Hooray, and up she rises
D
Hooray, and up she rises
Em
Hooray, and up she rises
Em D   Em
Ear-ly in the morning

[Verse]

Em
Put him in the bilge and make him drink it
D
Put him in the bilge and make him drink it
Em
Put him in the bilge and make him drink it

[Chorus]

Em D   Em
Ear-ly in the morning
Em
Hooray, and up she rises
D

Hooray, and up she rises
Em
Hooray, and up she rises
Em D   Em
Ear-ly in the morning

[Verse]

Em
Put him in a leaky boat and make him bale her
D
Put him in a leaky boat and make him bale her
Em
Put him in a leaky boat and make him bale her

[Chorus]

Em D   Em
Ear-ly in the morning
Em
Hooray, and up she rises
D
Hooray, and up she rises
Em
Hooray, and up she rises
Em D   Em
Ear-ly in the morning

[Verse]

Em
Tie him to the scuppers with the hose pipe on him
D
Tie him to the scuppers with the hose pipe on him
Em
Tie him to the scuppers with the hose pipe on him

[Chorus]

Em D   Em
Ear-ly in the morning
Em
Hooray, and up she rises
D
Hooray, and up she rises
Em
Hooray, and up she rises
Em D   Em
Ear-ly in the morning

[Verse]

Em
Shave his belly with a rusty razor
D
Shave his belly with a rusty razor
Em

Shave his belly with a rusty razor

[Chorus]

Em D   Em
Ear-ly in the morning
Em
Hooray, and up she rises
D
Hooray, and up she rises
Em
Hooray, and up she rises
Em D   Em
Ear-ly in the morning

[Verse]

Em
Tie him to the topmast while she's yardarm under
D
Tie him to the topmast while she's yardarm under
Em
Tie him to the topmast while she's yardarm under

[Chorus]

Em D   Em
Ear-ly in the morning
Em
Hooray, and up she rises
D
Hooray, and up she rises
Em
Hooray, and up she rises
Em D   Em
Ear-ly in the morning

[Verse]

Em
Heave him by the leg in a runnin' bowline
D
Heave him by the leg in a runnin' bowline
Em
Heave him by the leg in a runnin' bowline

[Chorus]

Em D   Em
Ear-ly in the morning
Em
Hooray, and up she rises
D

Hooray, and up she rises
Em
Hooray, and up she rises
Em D   Em
Ear-ly in the morning

[Verse]

Em
Keel haul him 'til he's sober
D
Keel haul him 'til he's sober
Em
Keel haul him 'til he's sober

[Chorus]

Em D   Em
Ear-ly in the morning
Em
Hooray, and up she rises
D
Hooray, and up she rises
Em
Hooray, and up she rises
Em D   Em
Ear-ly in the morning

Greensleeves

```
Am    C
Alas my love,
   G    Em
you do me wrong,
   Am          E
to cast me off so discourteously,
   Am    C    G    Em
for I have loved you so long,
   Am    E7    Am
delighting in your company.
```

[Chorus]

```
C           G    Em
greensleeves was all my joy,
Am          E
greensleeves was my delight,
C           G    Em
greensleeves was my heart of gold,
   Am       E7  Am
and who but my lady greensleeves.
```

[Verse 2]

```
   Am    C         G    Em
```

Thy gown was of the grassy green,
     Am   E
Thy sleeves of satin hanging by,
   Am   C   G   Em
Which made thee be our harvest queen,
  Am   E7   Am
And yet thou wouldst not love me.

[Chorus]

C   G   Em
greensleeves was all my joy,
Am   E
greensleeves was my delight,
C   G   Em
greensleeves was my heart of gold,
   Am   E7 Am
and who but my lady greensleeves.

[Verse 3]

  Am   C   G   Em
Well, I will pray to God on high,
     Am   E
That thou constancy mayst see,
   Am   C   G   Em
And that yet once before I die,
Am   E7   Am
Thou will vouchsafe to love me.

Jingle Bells

C
Dashing through the snow
           F
In a one horse open sleigh
             G
O'er the fields we go
               C
Laughing all the way
C
Bells on bob tails ring
               F
Making spirits bright
F   G
What fun it is to laugh and sing
G   C
A sleighing song tonight

C
Oh, jingle bells, jingle bells
C
Jingle all the way
F   C
Oh, what fun it is to ride
G
In a one horse open sleigh
C
Jingle bells, jingle bells
C
Jingle all the way

F   C
Oh, what fun it is to ride
G   (F)   C
In a one horse open sleigh

Chapter Nine: Stringing and Tuning Your Guitar

Playing the guitar when it has new strings is always a treat. The beautiful sounds of the strings and the quality of the notes make it seem as though you are playing a new instrument. However, fitting the little blighters is not such fun.

Remember, classical or Spanish guitars have nylon or gut strings, other varieties take steel strings. Put steel strings on a Spanish guitar and the stresses will be too much, resulting in damage to the body and neck.

If you are not going to be playing the guitar for a while, loosen the tension on the strings, it helps to take the pressure off the guitar's frame.

Restringing a Guitar

Little intricacies around the bridge can vary from guitar to guitar, but the basics are below.

Step One

Turn the tuning peg, loosening each of the existing strings, until all are quiet slack.

Step Two

Starting with the Low E string, keep loosening until the string can be pushed through its hole. Then, pull it out from the bridge. This may involve untying a knot, pulling by the little nut on the end of the string, or removing a string holder from the bridge by pulling, it will depend on your guitar.

Step Three

Repeat step two with all the other strings, starting with the A string, then through D, G, B and finishing with E.

Step Four

Take the bottom E string, the lowest note (it will be the thickest string, in its own little pack). Push the end through the hole in the bridge, and pull tight. Secure the string with whatever means the old string was secured by. Slide the string through the hole in its tuning peg, making sure that you have it in the correct peg. This first string will go through the first hole in the head at the top of the guitar.

Step Five

Pull the string tight, then feedback about 4-6 cm to create some slack.

Step Six

At the head end, angle the string slightly upwards and turn the tuning peg to tighten it. When the string is taught enough, position it in its slot in the nut of the guitar. That is the small, slotted strip where the neck meets the head. Tighten further until the string is sufficiently tense to remain in place in the nut. Don't worry about tuning yet.

Step Seven

Repeat steps four, five and six with the other strings, starting with the A string, then the D, G, B and finally the top E.

Step Eight

If you have excessive amounts of string hanging loose at the neck end, get some cutters and trim the strings. Leave about 3-4 cm showing.

You now have a restringed guitar…one that is very out of tune.

Tuning the Guitar

Unless you have purchased expensive, pre-stressed strings, then your guitar will go out of tune very quickly. You will need to retune regularly for a week or so. You will find that the guitar stays in tune for longer and longer periods.

First Tune

Unless you are blessed with perfect pitch, you will need something to tune the guitar to. A piano, tuning fork or measuring device attached to the head will do help you with this. Just as easy is to go online and search for a free guitar tuner. These work perfectly well.

Tuning the Guitar to itself

Once the instrument has settled after its re-stringing. It is much quicker to tune it to itself. This can be done in two ways.

Note Method

The fifth fret on the string is the same note as the open string on the next. So, pressing and playing the fifth fret on the A string, gives the note D, which is the same as the open D string.

The only exception is from the G string to the B string. Here, the fourth fret needs to be played to get the same note, B, as the open string after it.

Tune the string while holding down the note and letting both it and the open note ring on. Although requiring a bit of contortion, this allows you to hear the notes blend together.

Harmonic* Method

Harmonics are played by placing the finger of the left hand lightly on the string directly over a fret marker. The string is plucked and the finger lifted simultaneously. A bell like ringing sound is created.

Listening to the harmonics is a great way to tune, as rather than judging pitch, you will hear the vibrations of the harmonics. They will synch together when the notes are the same.

You will need to play harmonics on the fifth fret of the lower string, and seventh fret of the higher string to get the effect required. Unfortunately, this method does not work with the G to B strings, although it does with all other combinations.

Hearing Method

If you play a chord slowly, or two notes an octave* apart (use the table of notes in the earlier chapter to find where the same notes can be found) those with a good ear can hear whether their guitar is in tune or not. This gets easier with experience.

Tuning a Twelve String Guitar

If re-stringing a normal guitar is tricky, that is nothing to a 12 string. Tuning, too, is a little different.

For normal pitch, the main six strings are tuned as normal, but between each of the low E, A, D and G a string is fitted and pitched to an octave above the main note. The top two strings, B and top E, have their partners as identical pitch to themselves.

So, starting from the lowest string, the tuning is:

E (as per normal guitar)

E (up an octave)

A

A (up an octave)

D

D (up an octave)

G

G (up an octave)

B

B (same note, NOT up an octave)

E

E (same note, NOT up an octave)

Hard work, but a great sound.

Chapter Ten: Other Information

Types of Guitars

The main types are:

- *Spanish guitar*, usually the smallest kind, with nylon or gut strings, and a soft but precise sound. Usually finger picked, but can be strummed, usually with the thumb or fingers.
- *Acoustic Guitar*, steel stringed and usually finger picked or strummed with a plectrum.
- *Electric Acoustic*, as above with the addition of an electronic pick up to allow it to be played through an amplifier.
- *Electric Guitar*, often with one or two pick-ups, usually strummed or played as lead guitar – see below.
- *Bass Guitar*, four stringed electric with different tuning. Notes are usually plucked.
- *Combo*, a guitar with two necks allowing bass and normal guitar to be played.
- *Hollow Bodies Guitars* – these are electric guitars where the sound is enhanced with a hollow body. See below for an example.

- *Twelve String,* a steel strung acoustic usually strummed.
- *Hawaiian,* a guitar really in name only, although the steel tube with which the notes are formed can be bought for other guitar types.
- *Four and A Half String,* yes, really! Some of the earliest instruments were four stringed, with an extra, open string attached from the bridge to half way along the neck.

Looking After Your Guitar

You can get a decent, second hand model for $10, or you can pay thousands. Whichever, a guitar is a precision instrument and deserves to be treated as such. It is worth investing in a case to protect from everyday life. A soft one is fine if the guitar is to be kept at home, a hard one if it is going to be moved around, or the toddler can get access to it.

A soft, lint free duster can give the guitar a once over after it is played, removing finger marks, and specialist cleaners can be used to make it sparkle.

When the guitar is not in use, store it in a dry room, out of direct sunlight, away from a radiator and in a moderate temperature. Properly looked after, a guitar will last for life. In fact, for generations.

Buying a Guitar

Some things better with age. Cheese, fine red wine, Jane Fonda…many musical instruments also fit into this category. The guitar is no different. As the wood matures and settles, so the sound improves in quality. Therefore, there is no real need to buy new when $50 at a second hand will get a decent and very usable model. Double that for a new one.

But whether buying new or second hand, try out the instrument. Check that its weight is comfortable, and it is the right size. Elvis Presley played on a ¾ size instrument through the early part of his career, but he was a little special. Basically, make sure the guitar feels right when you hold it.

Check for cracks anywhere – if you find one walk away; a guitar is an instrument designed to take the stresses of tight strings, if there is a fault, it won't last for long. Check that there is no bowing on the back, and that the neck is straight.

Surface damage such as light scratches won't matter if they have not damaged the wood but if there are buzzes when played and the cause is not obvious (such as too much overhanging string at the head) then look elsewhere.

Make sure that the bridge is secure and the tuning parts are all in good condition.

Playing Lead

The lead guitarist is the quarter back, the centre forward, the Ferrari, the Tom Cruise of the guitar world. In other words, the glamour player. Listen to Pink Floyd or Dire Straits or Eric Clapton and hear the astonishing lead guitar melodies and riffs that take the music to that ultimate destination. Of course, just as Mr Cruise needs his support players and the quarterback (his team mates), so the lead is nothing without his rhythm back up.

But if lead is what you want, then a number of skills need to be developed. Some musical knowledge is needed, as lead improvisations come from an understanding of the constituent parts of the chord structure and key signatures being played.

Competency with both hands is needed. The left often picks notes at the end of the neck close to the body, where the frets are narrower, and more precision is needed. At the same time, picking notes with a plectrum is harder than doing it with the fingers.

But, as always, practice makes perfect and that starring role comes to those who want it and work for it.

If it is for you, start by grasping the first position. This is where notes are played using the first four frets, with the index finger on string one, and so forth ending with the little finger on fret four. Once tunes, melodies, harmonies and riffs* can be picked from here, then you can move on to working further down the fret board.

Accessories

Here is a list of some helpful accessories. Not all of these are required, so we have listed a usefulness factor after each. 1/5 means you may not need this item whereas 5/5 means you should have that item for playing regularly.

- *Stand* - frame for holding the guitar when it is not being used. It will add protection to the guitar and help preserve its life.   4/5
- *Footstool* – a handy device for serious Spanish guitar players and beginners as they get the guitar position right. To be honest, though, a pile of books works as well.   1/5

- *Plectrums and Picks* – essentials, especially plectrums, for the acoustic and electric guitar player. 5/5 (plectrums) 2/5 (finger picks)
- *Tuning Paraphernalia* – necessary in the old days, when a tuning fork was the only way to get into tune if there was no piano in the house. Nowadays it is all available online. 3/5 (because an portable tuner is always handy)
- *Metronome* – a handy tool for the beginner. A good, old fashioned metronome does the job and looks great, but as with tuning equipment, a metronome can be found for free through an app or online. 3/5 (but only for its decorative qualities)
- *Guitar Cover* – it will prolong the life of your instrument. 5/5
- *Strap* – depends on the type of guitar. Classical or Spanish guitars rarely come with strap holders as they are meant to be played sitting down. But if you have an electric, then you look a bit silly playing while sitting, at least if there is an audience. 3/5
- *Amplifier* – in the old days, your amp could double as a nuclear fallout shelter, so big and sturdy was the speaker. Now, for $50, a tiny amp capable of filling a large hall with sound is readily available. Pay more, and all kinds of effects will come as well. 5/5 for electric guitars.
- *Effects Pedals* – as spectacular as it looks, stamping on pedals while sweat pours of your face staining the silver lycra and making the Bowie Make Up run,

these are a bit, well, seventies. Just get a decent amp. 0/5

- *Music Stand* – from the mad to the sensible. A music stand will hold your music at the right level whether you stand or sit. Admittedly, a table also works, as does a chair and, if your eyesight is good enough, the floor. But, a music stands makes you look professional 2/5

Chapter Ten: Glossary – In Very Simplified Terms

Acoustic Guitar – Steel stringed and slightly larger than a classical guitar. Associated with folk music, some pop music. Ideal for strumming or picking.

Arpeggiated Chord – a chord where the individual notes are picked out one at a time.

Barre – Using the first finger to cover all six strings. This has the effect of allowing the basic chord shape to be played anywhere on the guitar neck. So, for example, the E shape creates the chord E when there is no barre. With a first fret barre, and the same shape after it, the chord moves up from an E to an F, one more and it becomes F#, next G, G#. A, A# (usually called Bb of B flat), C, C#, D, Eb (the same as D#) and then back to E.

Bass Guitar – Not covered in this book, but a four-stringed variety, with each string of a lower pitch than in the six-string variety, usually electric.

Chord – a combination of notes played together.

Classical Guitar – sometimes called Spanish Guitar, these are slightly smaller than other types usually. They are nylon stringed and can be used for classical music, finger picking and, sometimes, strumming.

Clef – the symbol in music which gives an indication of pitch. The guitar uses the treble clef, but never the bass clef. The clef appears at the beginning of a sheet of music.

Electric Guitar – Played through an amp. The easy action of electric guitars makes them comfortable to play. Ideal for lead or rhythm work. Less good for finger picking.

Finger Picking – playing notes individually, occasionally in pairs, with the thumb and fingers of the right (for right handed guitarists) hand.

Finger Style – see Finger Picking

Fret – The zones marked on the neck of the guitar. Each fret is marked by a narrow strip which runs perpendicular to and below the strings.

Fretboard – the frets on the neck of the guitar.

Hammer – playing a note by banging the left hand onto the string at the correct fret for the note.

Harmonics – bell like sounds played by placing the finger of the left hand lightly on the string directly above the fret marker. As the string is plucked, the finger lifts. A good place to practice is on the 12th fret for each string, where harmonics are easy to play.

Hawaiian Guitar – often played flat, they are tuned by using a hollow tube, which creates a unique, smooth and tropical sound. It is possible to buy the tubes and use them on other kinds of guitars.

Jamming, or Jam Session – informal playing with others.

Key – music is written in a 'key' – it tells you the combination of 'rules' that make the piece sound 'right'. The guitar is tuned to the key of E minor 7 with a suspension. There, that makes a lot of sense. It is possible to tune a guitar to a different key, but there are risks; the strings have a limit to which they can be stretched, and will snap if over tightened. Equally, if too slack, they will 'buzz' when played. It is best to stick in the natural key, which is changed through utilizing the frets and different chord placements.

Major Chords – those that sound full and complete.

Minor Chords – those chords that have a kind of questioning quality to them.

Notes – a note is the individual note that is made by playing a string. The notes change when the finger pushes down a string in a fret.

Octave – the group of eight notes between the same notes at different pitches. So, from C to C is an octave where D, E, F, G, A and B all fit between the two C notes.

Open String – this is the string when played with no notes pressed down on the frets. Starting from the string at the TOP of the guitar, the thickest string (which, confusingly, is the lowest note) they are E A D G B E.

Pick – sometimes called a plectrum, this is a triangular piece of thin plastic that comes in different widths – thin or light, medium and thick or heavy. It is used to strike the strings in an upwards or downward motion when strumming.

Plectrum – sometimes called a pick, this is a triangular piece of thin plastic that comes in different widths – thin or light, medium and thick or heavy. It is used to strike the strings in an upwards or downward motion when strumming.

Plucking – the action by which a note or notes are played by the right hand pulling the strings with a plucking action.

Pull off – a note played by the finger of the left hand pulling away from the string with a sharp, plucking action.

Riff – a repeated pattern of notes or chords.

Seventh Chords – a chord with an extra note.

Spanish Guitar - sometimes called Classical Guitar, these are slightly smaller than other types usually. They are nylon stringed and can be used for classical music, finger picking and, sometimes, strumming.

Strumming – the action of striking down the strings either with the thumb or plectrum (occasionally the first finger) when playing a chord.

Timbre – the musical quality of the sound created, often connected to mood and atmosphere.

Tuning or Tuned - these are the individual notes of the open strings. When played open (see above) they produce the following notes (see above). Starting from the string at the TOP of the guitar, the thickest string (which, confusingly, is the lowest note) they are E A D G B E.

Twelve String Guitars – as it suggests, twelve strings with clever tuning, creates a very full sound when strummed. Often used for country or folk type music.

Final Words

You have now reached the end of this introduction to the guitar. You could well be an expert player, about to organize your first gig in front of 1000 people at the local concert hall.

Much more likely is that practice, practice and more practice is what is needed next.

But competence will come quickly, given a bit of time. Twenty minutes a day will help you see rapid improvements in your playing and the acquisition of more and more skills.

Guitar playing is common, so it is easy to find advice from friends or the world wide web when you hit a problem. And that is a part of the joy of playing a guitar, or indeed any musical instrument.

You become a part of a community; a non-competitive, supportive and interesting one. There is enormous pleasure in playing your guitar by yourself, but even more by joining with others in a band, or just a friendly jam session* can be a lot of fun.

Make that your next step and now you are on the road to becoming a musician!